C0-ADW-236

The high-speed American racer Miss Stars & Stripes II.

The Story of
Man's Search
for Speed and
Distance

How Fast, How Far?

Adapted from the
original French text by
CLIFFORD PARKER
Illustrated by
GIANNINI

AMERICAN HERITAGE PRESS
NEW YORK

REVISED EDITION COPYRIGHT © 1969 BY AMERICAN HERITAGE PUBLISHING CO., INC.
COPYRIGHT © 1966 BY LES EDITIONS DES DEUX COQS D'OR, PARIS.
TRANSLATION COPYRIGHT © 1969 BY PAUL HAMLYN LTD.
ALL RIGHTS RESERVED.
LIBRARY OF CONGRESS CATALOG CARD NUMBER: 73-87001
SBN: 8281-5009-5 (trade)   8281-8009-1 (library)

Contents

CHAPTER ONE

Speed in Nature

The speed of a living creature has nothing to do with its size, strength, or intelligence. Man, for instance, is the most intelligent of all animals, and bigger and stronger than many of them. Yet, on his own two feet, he makes a poor showing on the scale of natural speeds. The fastest known living creature is, in fact, a small bird—the spine-tailed swift—whose flight has been reliably measured at 106 mph, and unofficial speeds of nearly 220 mph have been recorded.

The most fleet-footed of men have not yet reached 23 mph. Once in 1963, and three times in 1964, Bob Hayes of the United States ran the 100 yards in 9.1 seconds. But this speed cannot be taken as at all typical of a human being; it was achieved over a short distance on

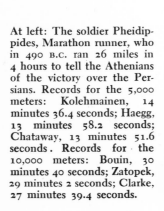

At left: The soldier Pheidippides, Marathon runner, who in 490 B.C. ran 26 miles in 4 hours to tell the Athenians of the victory over the Persians. Records for the 5,000 meters: Kolehmainen, 14 minutes 36.4 seconds; Haegg, 13 minutes 58.2 seconds; Chataway, 13 minutes 51.6 seconds. Records for the 10,000 meters: Bouin, 30 minutes 40 seconds; Zatopek, 29 minutes 2 seconds; Clarke, 27 minutes 39.4 seconds.

perfect running tracks by a highly trained athlete, and cost him a great deal of effort.

Since the organization of athletics at the end of the 19th century, running speeds have become much faster. Proper methods of training, coaching, diet, the concentration of a runner on a set distance, and, from time to time, the emergence of an athlete with superior natural ability, are resulting in better performances almost yearly. The gain each time has been small but measurable. And man has not yet reached his limits.

For nearly twenty-five centuries, the world marveled at the feat of the soldier Pheidippides, who ran in 4 hours more than 26 miles from the battlefield of Marathon to Athens with news of the Greek victory over the Persians. Phei-

dippides fell dead from exhaustion after giving the news. He was, of course, a soldier and not an athlete. The difference made by today's competition and training is shown in the present Marathon record of 2 hours 9 minutes 36.4 seconds set up by Derek Clayton at Fukuoka in Japan in 1967. Let us look at some world running records and see how the speed in miles per hour drops as the distance of the race increases. This, of course, is bound to happen. An athlete could not run for a mile and hope to keep up the speed he could reach in a sprint of 100 yards. Bob Hayes, as we have seen, ran 100 yards in 9.1 seconds, giving him a speed of almost 23 mph. Tommie Smith of the United States ran the 440 yards (a quarter mile) in 44.8 seconds, a speed of 20 mph. Peter Snell of New Zealand ran the 880 yards (a half mile) in 1 minute 45.1 seconds, almost 18 mph. In June, 1967, Jim Ryun, of the United States, ran the mile in 3 minutes 51.1 seconds, about 14 mph, clipping 0.2 seconds off his record of 3 minutes 51.3 seconds, set up in the previous year, when he broke the record held by the Frenchman, Michel Jazy. Ron Clarke of Australia ran the 3 miles in 12 minutes 50.4 seconds, almost 12 mph, and the 6 miles in 26 minutes 47 seconds. Ronald Hill of Great Britain ran 10 miles in 47 minutes 2 seconds and 15 miles in 1 hour 12 minutes 48.2 seconds.

In 1963, the New Zealander, William Bailey, ran for an hour and covered just over 12.5 miles. During the world's longest race—the 3,631 miles from New York to Los Angeles—run in 1929, the winner took 79 days to finish the course. Of this time, 526 hours were spent on the road, an average speed of nearly 7 mph. At this rate, it would take a year and a half to walk around the world.

An American, jumping from a balloon 102,200 feet high and opening his parachute at 17,500 feet from the ground, covered 16.04 miles in 4 minutes 38 seconds.

The limits of speed on a bicycle do not seem to have been reached yet. In 1928, a Belgian cyclist named Vanderstuyft covered 76 miles 504 yards in one hour, following a motorcycle. In 1962, a Frenchman, José Meiffret, reached a world speed record of 127.24 mph following a racing car fitted with a windshield. The fastest unpaced time is that of Antonio Maspes of Italy, who reached 42.21 mph by covering a 200-meter course in 10.6 seconds in 1962 at Milan;

but the official record is the 10.8 seconds made by Maspes in Rome in 1960.

Swimming is one of man's slowest means of getting about. He has not yet reached 5 mph unaided in water. The world's fastest swimming speed is the 4.89 mph set up in 1964 by Stephen Clark of the United States, but this was achieved over a distance of only 50 yards, which Clark covered in 20.9 seconds. In September, 1967, Zack Zorn of the United States set up a time of 52.6 seconds for the 100-meter free style race, a speed of 4 mph. In 1960, Jon Konrads, Australia, set up a time of 17 minutes 11 seconds for a swim of 1,650 yards, a speed of 3.5 mph. The fastest time for swimming the 21 miles across the Strait of Dover in the English Channel is 9 hours 35 minutes, set up in 1964 by the English swimmer Barry Watson, who crossed from Cap Gris-Nez, France, to Dover. The record for crossing from England to France is held by Nitindra Naragan of India, who in 1967 crossed in a time of 10 hours 21 minutes. The fastest double crossing was made in 1965 by Ted Erikson of the United States, who swam from Dover to Calais and back in 30 hours 3 minutes.

Champions on roller skates can travel just over 20 mph for short distances, but for a mile, they can pick up speed, and they can travel just under 24 mph. The German, Jurgen Traub, skated a mile in 2 minutes 26.8 seconds in 1966. The world record for the greatest distance skated in one hour is, surprisingly, the women's world record, held by C. Patricia Barnett, who managed to cover a distance of 20 miles 1,355 yards in the hour.

Speeds on ice and snow are fast indeed. A bobsled can reach more than 80 mph. On ice skates, over a mile, champion skaters reach almost 25 mph.

The highest reliable recorded speed on skis is that of Erhard Keller of Germany, who covered 500 meters in 39.2 seconds in Germany in 1968, a speed of 28.5 mph.

Man can reach his fastest unaided speed simply by falling from a great height. An American parachutist who jumped from a balloon at a height of 102,200 feet and opened his parachute only 17,500 feet from the ground, fell 84,700 feet (16.04 miles) in 4 minutes 38 seconds, reaching a speed of more than 220 mph.

Even eating and drinking have their speed records. A roast ox was eaten by one man in 42 days; 56 raw eggs were eaten in 2 minutes; 44 boiled eggs were eaten in 30 minutes; 2.5 pints of ale were drunk in 6.5 seconds; and 40 bananas were eaten in 39 minutes.

Supple hands and quick reflexes are needed for speed records in shorthand and typing. Shorthand records are 300 words a minute for 5 minutes, 350 words a minute for 2 minutes, and 50,000 words in 5 hours. The unofficial typing record, on an electric machine, is 216 words per minute. The official record for an hour is 149 words per minute. On a nonelectric machine, the official records are 170 words in one minute, and 147 words per minute for an hour's typing. The highest speed for sending Morse code is 75 words per minute, or more than 17 symbols per second.

Man's reflexes themselves have been measured for speed. The nervous system can send a message to the brain at 265 mph. Hair grows about a half inch every 30 days. A good pianist must be able to read 1,500 notes a minute and make, at the same time, 2,000 movements of the hands. To play some parts of an *étude* by Chopin, he has to read 3,950 notes in 2.5 minutes, and to play the *Mouvement Perpétuel* by Weber he must read 4,541 notes in less than 4 minutes. Even creative writing has been timed. The fastest novel writer in the world is Erle Stanley Gardner, creator of the famous Perry Mason. He writes seven novels, all at the same time, and dictates up to 10,000 words a day.

Speed in the Animal Kingdom

For sheer speed, many animals leave man far behind. We have already noted the performance of the spine-tailed

The Austrian Toni Sailer, one of the best skiers of the world. The highest speed reached on skis is 108.59 mph.

Many animals are speedier than man. Above: The spine-tailed swift, 106 mph. Right: The ostrich, which can run up to 50 mph. Below: The partridge flies up to 75 mph, even when turning in mid-air.

swift, which has a measured speed of 106 mph. The peregrine falcon has a speed of 185 mph when diving down at its prey. The highest average speed for a bird in level flight over a long distance is that of a carrier pigeon that covered 186 miles at 97.40 mph. An eagle can travel at about this speed, while some ducks and geese can reach 70 mph. At top speed, an ostrich can run 50 mph and the emu up to 40 mph.

Fastest among the mammals is the cheetah, which can travel at 60 mph for short distances. The cheetah's endurance is not great, however; over a two-mile course, its average speed is about 45 mph.

The top speed of a racehorse is 43.26 mph. A speed of 43 mph is claimed for the saluki, but actually the fastest dog is probably the greyhound, which can reach a measured speed of 39 mph.

The fastest reptile on land is the race runner lizard of the southern United States, which has been timed at 18 mph. The fastest snake is the black mamba, which can keep up a steady 7 mph and reach 15 mph for short distances. Stories have been told of mambas overtaking galloping horses, but this seems to be stretching the truth a little.

The slowest reptile is the tortoise. Even the biggest, a Mauritian giant tortoise, could not move faster than five yards a minute (0.17 mph) when it was galloping hungrily after a juicy cabbage. The slowest of all animals is, of course, the snail, with a bottom speed of 23 inches per hour and a top speed of 55 yards per hour. The shrimp has a speed of 386 yards per hour; the caterpillar, 73 yards per hour; and the earthworm 18 yards per hour. The fastest recorded speed for a spider is 1.17 mph.

Fastest of all the fish is undoubtedly the swordfish, which has been credited

The peregrine falcon: the speed with which it plunges down at its prey has been timed at 185 mph.

with speeds of between 57 and 68 mph. The pike can reach nearly 10 mph; the flying fish can leap through the air at nearly 50 mph; the trout can swim at 5 to 15 mph; and a 200-pound salmon can keep up a speed of almost 10 mph for 20 seconds.

Claims of fantastically high speeds for flying insects are now looked upon as doubtful. The dragonfly *Austrophlebia* was reported to fly at between 55 and 60 mph. Experiments, however, show that the fastest any insect flies normally is 24 mph, with short bursts of up to 36 mph. After the dragonfly, the fastest insects include: the gadfly (30 mph), the bee (18 mph), the wasp (12 mph), the cockchafer (6 mph), the housefly (5 mph), the mosquito (3 mph), and the mayfly (just over 1 mph). Of the two divisions of lepidoptera, the fastest moths can fly at 33 mph and the

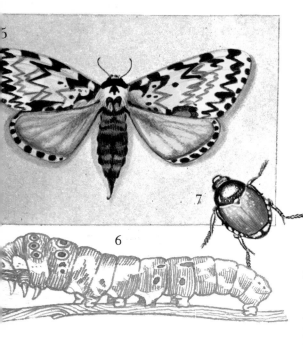

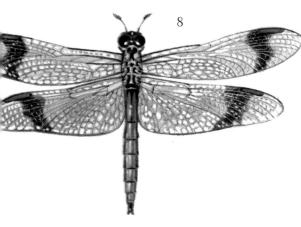

Some speeds in the animal world:
1. Swordfish, 57 mph.
2. Flying fish, 50 mph.
3. Trout, 5 to 15 mph.
4. Pike, 10 mph.
5. Butterfly, 20 mph.
6. Caterpillar, 73 yards per hour.
7. Cockchafer, 6 mph.
8. Dragonfly, 36 mph.
9. Giant tortoise, 300 yards per hour.
10. Race runner lizard, 18 mph.
11. Black mamba, 7 mph.
12. Snail, 55 yards per hour.

fastest butterflies at 20 mph. The fastest wingbeat of any insect is that of the midge *Forcipomyia*, with 57,000 beats per minute.

In the microscopic world of the protozoa, the ameba does not even reach a speed of half an inch an hour. Another protozoan, however, the *Monas stigmatica*, can move a distance equal to 40 times its own length in a second—a feat equivalent to the impossible one of a man six feet tall covering 240 feet in a second.

The partnership between man and the horse has been a long one, and before the invention of the locomotive, the horse was man's principal means of getting about at any speed faster than his own. Horse racing over the centuries has resulted in the breeding of superb fast animals.

Horse racing today is a major sport and industry in many countries, with Britain, France, and the United States in the lead. All present racehorses are descended from three Arab stallions—Darley Arabian, Godolphin Arabian, and Byerly Turn, brought to England in the late 17th century. At the beginning of the 18th century, racehorses began to achieve times unheard of before. The great horse Eclipse, foaled in 1764, was never beaten. The French began to catch up in the 19th century; in 1865, the French horse Gladiateur won the British Triple Crown (the 2,000 Guineas, the Derby, and the St. Leger) *and* the Ascot Gold Cup.

The present top speed is the 43.26 mph achieved by the American racehorse Big Racket, over a quarter of a mile. Record speed for a mile is the 39.21 mph on a partly downhill course achieved by the British Soueida. In the early 18th century a horse called Flying Childers was said to have run the dis-

tance of a mile in one minute, but no official record exists.

Speed in the Vegetable Kingdom

Speed is perhaps not the word to apply to the growth of plants. But movement is there, growth is there, in even the most ordinary and apparently immobile plant.

Several trees grow at a rate of only 0.14 inch per year. The *Eucalyptus saligna*, in central Africa, grows at the rate of more than 44 feet in two years. Bamboo, which is really a grass, grows in Ceylon at a speed of 18 inches in a day until it reaches a height of more than 100 feet. Another grass, the *Puya raimondii*, has the double distinction of growing at one of the highest altitudes (between 12,000 and 13,000 feet up in the Andes) and of being the most slow-growing grass. This grass is 150 years old before it flowers. About 8,000 white

The horse Gladiateur, bred in France, did very well on the British race fields in the 19th century.

The cheetah is the fastest mammal. It can average a speed of 45 mph, and over short distances it can reach 60 mph.

flowers open on an enormous stem, more than 6 feet in diameter and more than 30 feet tall. This spectacular blossoming, however, heralds the end of the plant's long life; once the seeds have ripened, it dies.

Speeds of Some Meteorological Phenomena

Storms give us some of the fastest natural speeds on earth. In cyclones the wind roars around at several hundred miles per hour. The cyclone itself moves along more slowly at 21 mph in the

Racing greyhounds are probably the fastest dogs. Over a race course, they can reach 39 mph.

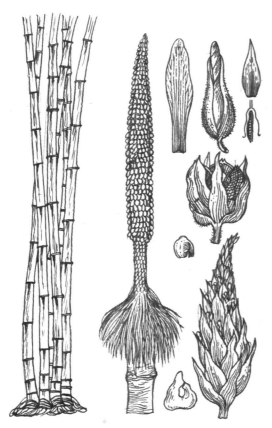

Left: Bamboo stalks. Right: *Puya raimondii*, the slowest flowering plant in the world, grows on the summits of the Andes between 12,000 and 13,000 feet up; it is 150 years old before the 8,000 flowers bloom on its 30-foot-tall stem.

Caribbean and 12 mph in the China Sea. The sandstorms caused by the harmattan, a dry wind of Western Africa, can be 3,300 feet high and cover hundreds of miles at a speed of almost 22 mph.

The Beaufort Scale, which is used to describe the force of the wind, gives as Force 12—hurricane—any wind over 75 mph. A mere 75 seems slow compared with the top recorded wind speeds. The highest was the 280 mph wind recorded at Wichita Falls, Kansas, in 1938. Tornado winds at their fastest exceed 200 mph. During a tornado in 1842 in Mayfield, Kansas, the winds were believed to have reached 620 mph. Winds in the higher reaches of the atmosphere exceed 400 mph. On the earth's surface, the wind blows strongest at Commonwealth Bay, near the magnetic South Pole. The windiest place in the United States is Mount Washington, New Hampshire, which has a yearly average of 35.6 mph. The least windy places in the United States are Chat-

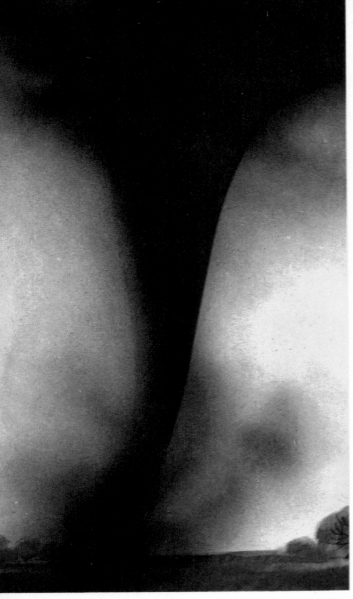

The tornado itself moves slowly, but the winds within it often blow several hundred miles an hour.

tanooga, Tennessee, and San Diego, California, which both have averages of 6.4 mph.

The strongest water currents in the world are those of Saltfjord, in Norway, where they reach 18.4 mph. River "bores" (tidal waves that run up a river) can reach quite high speeds. The bore in the Tsien Tang Kiang in Eastern China reaches a height of up to 25 feet and a speed of 13 knots. The bore on one of the branches of the Ganges Delta in India reaches more than 15 knots and travels for 70 miles. Tidal waves caused by earthquakes or landslides are sometimes between 60 and 100 feet high and can travel across the seas at speeds of up to 490 mph. Avalanches of snow can reach great speeds. In 1890, in Garmisch-Partenkirchen in the Bavarian Alps, one came down a 44-degree slope at 190 mph.

Here are some interesting random figures: In astronomy, the cosmic year represents 200 million earthly, or terrestrial, years. The slowest clock mechanism is that of the Town Hall of Copenhagen. The hand showing the movement of the celestial pole will take 25,700 years to go around the dial. The length of a day increases at the rate of 0.00117 milliseconds a day, or 0.0427 seconds in a century.

The fastest camera in the world is one at the Atomic Weapons Research Establishment at Aldermaston, Berkshire, in England. It makes 60 million exposures a second. The fastest known rotating speed is the 1,500,000 revolutions a second made by the steel rotor suspended in a vacuum in an ultracentrifuge in the Rouss Physical Laboratory at the University of Virginia. The fastest type-setting machine in the world is the I.B.M. 1403 model used in conjunction with computers. It can set 1,100 lines of 132 letters each in a minute, or 1,400 lines of numbers.

In New York City are the world's fastest nonindustrial passenger elevators. They carry people up and down the skyscrapers at 15.9 mph, or 1,400 feet a minute. In the South African mines the elevators travel at up to 41 mph.

CHAPTER TWO

Speed of Sound, Light and Projectiles

Man's need to determine the speed of sound and light has been the driving force behind some of his most thrilling research and has resulted in many remarkable discoveries. One of the main aims of this research has been swifter communication—a means of transmitting news and information faster than a horse could gallop or a carrier pigeon could fly.

Julius Caesar mentions in his Commentaries one early means of rapid communication. "When anything extraordinary happened, the Gauls signaled with loud cries, which were heard from one place to the other: in such a way, the massacre of the Romans which happened in Orléans at dawn, was known at nine o'clock in the evening at Auvergne, 40 leagues away."

Tribes of Central Africa send messages in a similar way by beating tom-toms, the "talking drums."

We know today that sound travels at different speeds through different mediums. It travels through air, when the temperature is at freezing point (32 degrees F.), at 1,100 feet per second, or 750 mph. The speed increases as the temperature rises by a foot per second for each degree Fahrenheit. Sound is affected by the density and elasticity of the medium through which it is traveling. The denser the medium, the slower the speed; the more elastic, the faster. Water is denser than air but much more elastic; sound travels through water at 4,700 feet per second. In a vacuum, sound does not travel at all because there is no medium for it to travel through.

The speed of sound is the unit used to measure the speed of supersonic aircraft. It is called Mach, after the Austrian physicist Ernst Mach. Mach 1 is the speed of sound; Mach 2 is twice the speed, and so on.

Long before electricity came into use, man realized that light was speedier than sound for sending messages.

First experiments on the speed of sound in air, in 1822. The interval between the flash of the shot and hearing its sound was measured quite accurately; at 32 degrees F., 1,086 feet per second was recorded.

The first machines of war were catapults that threw heavy objects, often stones fashioned in the form of balls.

From ancient times, relays of fire were used to signal pre-arranged messages. King Agamemnon was said to have signaled the fall of Troy to his queen, Clytemnestra, by a succession of bonfires. In many countries, special beacons were built so that fires lighted on top of them could be seen many miles away.

In 1774, a Swiss scientist, Georges-Louis Lesage, invented the first electric telegraph—but unfortunately, nobody was interested in the idea! The apparatus was made up of 24 wires corresponding to letters of the alphabet. At the end of each wire was suspended a little ball of elder pith. When one end of the wire was touched with an electrified glass rod, the ball at the other end jerked, so indicating a letter.

A very effective visual telegraph, or semaphore, was invented in the early

Mounted on a small but swift pony, the Asiatic horseman, with his bow and quiver of arrows, was a redoubtable foe in Eastern Europe during the 4th and 5th centuries.

The crossbow, one of the most powerful weapons from the Middle Ages to the Renaissance. In the battle of Crécy, in 1346, the bolts of the Genoese archers pierced the armor of the French knights at a range of more than 300 feet.

1790s by Claude Chappe; it sent messages for miles across France at speeds never before dreamed of. Such progress, however, was not accepted without opposition. Mobs twice smashed Chappe's apparatus. The first time they believed it to be witchcraft. The second time they accused Chappe of using it to send secret messages between Louis XVI, who had been imprisoned by the revolutionists, and his supporters. The apparatus was simply an upright, at the top of which three arms were moved by pulleys. The positions of the arms corresponded in code to various letters of the alphabet.

If the names of Ampère, Œrsted, Arago, and Faraday are linked with the study and development of the electric telegraph, the name of Samuel Morse will be forever connected with the code named after him and the hand-operated key transmitter-receiver by which it was sent. On May 24th, 1844, Morse sent over his new telegraph line from Washington, D.C., to Baltimore the words "What hath God wrought!" In Baltimore, his assistant, Alfred Vail, took down the message and tapped it out back to Washington. In the next year the Washington-Baltimore line was opened for public use, and soon many newspapers were using the new system.

Britain, meanwhile, already had the beginnings of a telegraph system. In 1837, William F. Cooke and Charles Wheatstone devised an instrument in which magnetic needles pointed to the letter of the alphabet signaled. First installed in 1838 on the London and Blackwall Railway, the system was used in Britain until 1870. France's first telegraphic network was opened

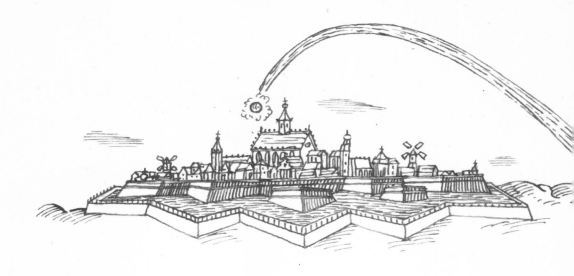

in 1851 and linked to Britain's by an undersea cable. On August 12th, 1858, the first transatlantic cable carried a message from Queen Victoria to President James Buchanan of the United States.

In 1801, it took 21 days for the news of the murder of Paul I, Czar of Russia, to reach London from Moscow. In 1855, the news of the death of Czar Nicholas took only 4 hours and 15 minutes to arrive.

In March, 1867, a message sent from London at the close of the Stock Exchange at 4 P.M. arrived in New York at noon on the same day! Though it appeared that the message had been received before it had been sent, it was, of course, due to the different time zones in which the two cities lie.

Once the telegraph had paved the way, speed in transmission of messages became more and more rapid. Today, with the telephone, radio, and television, communication is almost instantaneous, as easy and quick as talking to somebody in the same room. Across the world, and across space, messages are flashing at the speed of light, which is 186,282 miles per second, or 670,615,200 mph.

Speed of Projectiles

Weapons have been indispensable to man, who has used them from the beginning for offense and defense, against wild animals and against his fellow men. The first war ever fought was undoubtedly over the possession of hunting grounds or water holes. And the winners were almost certainly the side with the best weapons and the greatest skill in using them.

The technique that above all others has made man supreme as a fighting animal is that of ballistics—hurling an object through the air. Hand-to-hand fighting became much less important, and man became powerful far beyond his own strength and agility, once he was able to fight his foe from a distance.

From the boomerang, the sling, the javelin, and the blowpipe, through the first firearms, and right up to the nu-

Used mainly during sieges, bombards, ancestors of the cannon, were short tubes of metal placed on a chassis without wheels. They were often used to fire incendiary balls.

clear missile, man has made his weapons progressively speedier to operate, more accurate over longer distances, and more destructive in their effect.

With the ballistas and catapults of old, the bow and then the crossbow, speeds increased more and more. The arrow at first replaced the stone, but the stone rapidly regained its former importance, simply because of its weight, as machines were invented that could throw heavy stones long distances. Stone balls were fired from the bombards (the first cannons) when they appeared in Europe around 1250. By the mid-1300s these bombards were being made small enough to be carried and fired by one man. From these first handguns, called arquebuses, came the musket, the pistol, and in time the rifle and revolver of today.

After gunpowder replaced muscle-power, the science of ballistics became a more precise one. Yet several centuries went by before theories were established about the relationship between muzzle velocity (the speed at which the projectile leaves the barrel) and the range of the projectile. During the early 17th century, when France was involved in the Thirty Years' War, it was calculated that the range of a cannon ball fired with a muzzle velocity of 1,500 feet per second was twice as great as one fired at 1,000 feet per second.

Large modern guns shoot out shells at speeds of from 800 to 3,000 feet per second. High-powered rifles can discharge a bullet at 7,100 feet per second. The effectiveness of modern guns, as well as their range, depends on the *rate* at which the projectile can be fired. Two things that greatly increased the rate of fire in the mid-1800s were the development of breech-loading (loading from the breech instead

Appearing in the 15th century, the match arquebus of the infantry was used for a period of 250 years. Both ends of the match were kept lit in case either of them went out.

Modern machine guns can fire between 400 and 1,500 rounds per minute. The world's fastest gun is the 30 mm Vulcan cannon, fitted in aircraft such as the F-105; it can fire 6,000 rounds per minute, or a hundred rounds per second!

The ordinary shell, like all other projectiles, has two drawbacks. It is slowed down rapidly by air resistance once it leaves the gun, and it can be stopped by thick armor plate. Man's ingenuity has overcome both these problems. Some shells carry a windshield, a sharply pointed false nose, to cut down air resistance. Armor-piercing shells, with tough, pointed noses and thick cases have been developed to punch through metal or concrete. Ponderous, heavily armored ships and tanks are practically useless today. Modern fighting craft rely for their safety on speed and mobility.

Modern fighter planes are fitted with rocket-propelled missiles instead of ordinary cannon. One good reason for this is that many of the planes can fly faster than the cannon shells they fire! In 1962, an American Crusader fighter on an exercise actually caught up with its own shells, which had been slowed down by air resistance.

Just as the rocket is more effective than the ordinary shell, so the guided missile is faster and more effective than ordinary rockets. These missiles, powered by the rocket engines, carry an electronic brain to guide them. The simplest are the ballistic missiles, which are guided only for the first part of their flight, after which they drop on a fixed trajectory like an artillery shell. The nonballistic missiles use many kinds of complicated devices, including radar, infrared heat detectors, sound detectors, and computers, to guide

of from the muzzle) and the cartridge, in which powder, detonator, and bullet were all in one. In America, early repeating rifles, such as the Winchester 73 and the Colt Lightning, fired two or three shots a second. Skilled riflemen today can fire more than 20 aimed rounds per minute with an ordinary bolt-action rifle. With automatic rifles, which the rifleman can fire without loading between every shot, between 40 and 60 aimed shots per minute can be fired. Automatics can also be fired in short bursts like a machine gun.

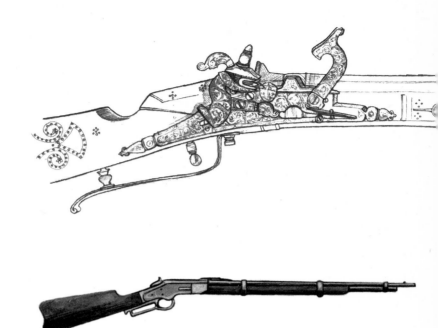

The chenapan, a flintlock manufactured in the 15th century for the hunting gun of the King of England and Scotland, Charles I, was the most rudimentary system of firing with flint.

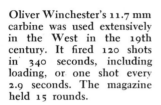

Oliver Winchester's 11.7 mm carbine was used extensively in the West in the 19th century. It fired 120 shots in 340 seconds, including loading, or one shot every 2.9 seconds. The magazine held 15 rounds.

them all the way to the target at speeds of more than 10,000 mph. There are many sizes of guided missiles, ranging from small ones used as infantry weapons to giant spacecraft.

Cosmic Speeds

The first measurement of the speed of light was made in 1675 by Olaüs Rœmer, a Danish astronomer. He concluded that it took 16 minutes for light to travel across the diameter of the earth's path around the sun, and he worked out its speed at 192,000 miles per second. In 1930, the American scientist Albert Michelson measured the speed of light in a vacuum at 186,-284 miles per second. Since then it has been fixed more accurately at 186,282 miles per second. Rœmer, almost 300 years ago, was not so far wrong.

The light that our eyes can see is only a small part of the electromagnetic energy given off by the sun. The electromagnetic waves—radio, ultraviolet, infrared, X rays, and gamma rays—travel at the same speed as visible light. This speed is not always constant; in a vacuum it is 186,282 miles per second; in air it is a little less; and through transparent substances, such as glass or water, it is much less. This difference in speed causes the bending, or refraction, of light when it passes at an angle through glass or water. This is why a paint brush standing in a jar of water appears to be bent. It is also the reason why a glass prism can separate light into its different colors.

Though the stars at night seem so still when we look up at the sky, everything in our universe is moving very fast indeed. Meteorites travel at more than 40 miles per second.

The earth goes around the sun at a rate of 18.5 miles per second and turns on its axis at a speed of 662 mph at the

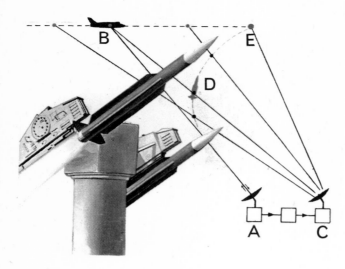

A ground-to-air missile intercepting an airplane by radar guidance. The radar (A) catches the airplane (B) in its beam and orients a range-finder (C), which works out the exact position of the enemy and directs the missile (D) while correcting its flight; the missile meets the objective in flight at (E).

equator. Mercury rotates on its axis once every 88 days—the same time it takes to orbit the sun—at a speed of 31 miles per second. It takes Venus 225 days to go around the sun; Mars, two years; Jupiter, 12 years; Saturn, 29.5 years; Uranus, 84 years; Neptune, 165 years; and Pluto, 248 years. Though these journeys take such a long time, the speeds traveled are unbelievably fast.

Will man ever reach, or even exceed, the "light barrier"? It has been calculated that an existing rocket would need to accelerate constantly for 40 days to reach the speed of light. After that, it seems, time would disappear for the passengers, and nothing would prevent them from landing on worlds millions of light years away. (A light year is the distance light travels in one year—6,000,000,000,000 miles.)

One writer has imagined a traveler leaving the earth at a speed approaching the speed of light and returning two years later at the same speed, to find that the earth was not two years older, but two centuries older.

According to Einstein's Theory of Relativity, and to what other knowledge we have, the speed of light is an *absolute* speed, which means that it can never be exceeded. It is possible to prove that absolute zero exists in temperature, at minus 459.6 degrees Fahrenheit. But Einstein's theory of the absolute speed of light cannot yet be proven. Some scientists think that certain phenomena point to the possibility of there being higher speeds than that of light. The effects of gravity, for instance, might be felt over a given distance much more quickly than light could travel. As yet, however, man has not learned to measure even the approximate speed of this action.

The Soviet bomber Myasishchev Bounder, 1959 (620 mph, ceiling, 51,000 feet), escorted by 2 MIG 21 fighters (Mach 2, ceiling, 59,000 feet).

CHAPTER THREE

Speed on the Road

The Invention of the Wheel

For many thousands of years, man could travel on land only as fast as his own two feet could carry him. Even today there are peoples in remote parts of the world, in the thick jungles of the Amazon and the interior of New Guinea, for instance, who have no other means of transport.

Long ago, however—and nobody knows for certain how long—man discovered how to harness the speed and strength of certain animals, how to tame them, and how to put their speed and strength to his own use. For speed, he used swift-footed animals like the horse, the camel, and even, in the case of the Eskimo, the dog. Where sheer strength was needed, he taught the ox, the water buffalo, and the elephant to pull his plow and haul his loads.

Great as these advances were, man's progress to our present state of civilization would not have been possible without the invention of the first and most important aid to mechanical propulsion —the wheel. The wheel was invented five and a half thousand years ago by the Sumerians, who lived in the land between the rivers Tigris and Euphrates in Mesopotamia. This land, now part of Iraq, was the cradle of our civilization. The Sumerians invented the first system of writing, had a knowledge of medicine, mathematics, astronomy, and a well developed system of agriculture. Once they had invented the wheel, which at first was just a solid block of wood, they kept on improving it, rimming it first with leather and then bronze tires. The Babylonians further improved the wheel by cutting out parts of the wooden disc to make it lighter. About 2000 B.C., chariots with spoked wheels appeared in the Middle East. Still, however, vehicles could go no faster than the animal that pulled them. And it was not until the first half of the 19th century, when a light-bodied, two-wheeled vehicle appeared, that any appreciable gain in speed was made. That vehicle was the bicycle.

The Bicycle

A 17th-century stained-glass window in an English church shows an angel moving through the clouds, sitting in a two-wheeled machine very like a bicycle. This was a strangely prophetic picture, for the first bicycle did not appear until more than a century later, in 1790, when the French nobleman, Comte de Sivrac, invented the *célérifère*. This was simply a wooden frame with a wheel at either end. The rider sat astride the frame and pushed the ground with his feet. There was no steering, and the rider had to lean in the direction he wanted to turn. Later models of the machine were called *vélocifères*.

In 1816, the German Baron von Drais experimented with a machine named

27

The evolution of the bicycle from 1818 to today: (1) The draisine, invented by Baron de Drais in 1818. (2) The high-wheeler, 1870s, whose front wheel reached up to 6.5 feet in diameter. (3) and (4) Two chain-driven models used in the 19th century. (5) Modern racing bicycle. (6) Record-breaking bicycle with aerodynamic body.

after him, the draisine. This machine was still pushed by the feet, but it could be steered. In England it became known as the "dandy," or "hobby horse." A Scottish blacksmith, Kirkpatrick Macmillan, made the first pedal-driven machine in 1839. The pedals were pushed backward and forward and worked rods attached to the back wheel. In the early 1860s, the Frenchman Pierre Michaux and his son, Ernest, produced a machine driven by pedals on the hub of the front wheel. This machine, the *vélocipède* was nicknamed the "boneshaker." Other improvements followed rapidly, such as Tribout's ball bearings. Cycling became popular in England, and the front wheel grew larger until, by the 1880s, the famous "penny-farthing" was being used. Improvements were being made constantly. In 1873, H. J. Lawson patented his safety bicycle, which had a chain drive to the rear wheel. In 1879, the Bayliss Thomas bicycle, with bearings in the wheels, made its appearance. In 1888, John Boyd Dunlop fitted a bicycle with the first pneumatic tires.

By the 1890s, cycling was very popular in Europe and in the United States, where 4,000,000 people regularly rode

bicycles. But bicycle racing has always been more popular in England and Europe than in the United States.

The most famous bicycle race in the world is undoubtedly the Tour de France, a grueling ride around France that takes more than three weeks to complete. The longest Tour de France was held from June 20th to July 18th, 1926, when the riders had to cover 3,569 miles!

Comparison of figures will give some idea of the progress of riders and the improvements in machines over the years. During the first race from Paris to Brest and back, in 1891, 750 miles were covered in 71 hours 30 minutes. In 1921, the Belgian Louis Mottiat won the same race in 55 hours 7 minutes 8 seconds; in 1948, Albert Hendrick of Belgium did it in 41 hours 36 minutes 42 seconds; in 1951, Maurice Diot of France took only 38 hours 55 minutes 45 seconds. In 1908, Petit-Breton won the Tour de France with an average of 17 mph. In 1964, Jacques Anquetil averaged 22 mph.

British cycling records include 52 minutes 28 seconds for 25 miles (Dave Dungworth, 1966); 1 hour 48 minutes 33 seconds for 50 miles (Pete Smith,

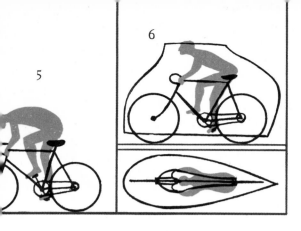

5

6

1967); and 3 hours 51 minutes 41 seconds for 100 miles (Martyn Roach, 1968). Time records include the 276.55 miles covered in 12 hours by Mike Mc-Namara in 1967 and the 496.37 miles in 24 hours covered by Nim Carline in 1966. In 1965, Richard Poole cycled the 871 miles from Land's End to John o'Groats in 1 day 23 hours 46 minutes.

The world record for one hour on a track without a pacer is the 29.88 miles covered by Ferdinand Bracke of Belgium in 1967. The cyclist paced and shielded from the wind by another vehicle can make almost unbelievable times. In Chapter One we mentioned the 76 miles 504 yards covered in one hour by the Belgian Leon Vanderstuyft, and the speed of 127.24 mph reached behind a racing car by the French cyclist José Meiffret.

The Motorcycle

Quite early in the history of the bicycle, manufacturers had the idea of fitting it with an engine, both to increase the speed and to save effort on the part of the rider. In 1868, the French engineer M. Perrot fitted a Michaux bicycle with an engine. In 1884, the Englishman Edward Butler built a two-cylinder motorcycle at the same time as Gottlieb Daimler was trying out his gasoline engine on a bicycle in Germany. World War I saw the motorcycle really come into its own, and its popularity soared in the years immediately afterward. In September, 1966, Robert Leppan of the United States set a world motorcycle speed record of 245.67 mph on a machine powered by two 650 cc Triumph engines and run on alcohol. The longest distance covered in one hour is 144.83 miles, achieved in 1964 by the Englishman Mike Hailwood on an American speedway track. The most famous motorcycle race in the world is probably the Isle of Man Senior Tourist Trophy Race. It is also the longest (37.73 miles) and the trickiest, with 264 bends and corners. Fastest average speed for this is 105.62 mph, again achieved by Hailwood in 1967.

The Fardier, designed by Nicolas Cugnot, was the first automobile; built in 1769, this steam-driven vehicle carried four people at a speed of 2 mph.

Steam car built by the engineer Richard Trevithick; in 1802, it reached 9 mph.

The Automobile

The world's first motor vehicle was the Fardier, a lumbering steam carriage built by Nicolas Joseph Cugnot, a French army officer, in 1769. It carried four people at a speed of 2 mph but could not run for more than 12 minutes and overturned on its second test run. Not a very promising beginning, perhaps, but the automobile had become a reality. The French War Minister asked Cugnot to build another machine, this time to carry a load of four to five tons at a speed of 2.5 mph. This Cugnot did, and a second Fardier took to the road between November, 1770 and July, 1771. Forgotten in the turmoil of the French Revolution, the Fardier now stands rebuilt in a museum in Paris.

Several steam carriages were tried out in England in the early 19th century. Richard Trevithick built one which, in 1802, traveled from Camborne to Plymouth and reached all of 9 mph on the level! Sir Goldsworth Gurney built a machine which, in 1829, covered the 200 miles from London to Bath at an average speed of 15 mph. Between 1831 and 1836, a man named Hancock built nine steam buses and set up a regular service. People were a little frightened of the new machines and at first customers were all too rare. By 1836, however, twenty steam carriages were running on the roads of Britain. The stagecoach and railway companies feared the competition, and their efforts helped to push through a law in 1865 that made it illegal for a self-propelled vehicle to use the road unless a man with a red flag walked in front. The speed, moreover, was not to exceed 4 mph. This law, which was not changed until 1896, when the red flag was abolished and the speed limit raised to 14 mph, delayed the development of the automobile in Britain.

More than fifty years after the Fardier, experiments in steam traction began again in Europe. Road-trains,

This vehicle, with horizontal boiler and three wheels, was used on French experimental lines starting in 1867.

The Automaton, 20-seat omnibus, ran in England between Moorgate and Paddington from 1836 to 1840 at 15.5 mph.

consisting of a locomotive pulling several carriages, were built by Jean-Christian Dietz and his son, Charles. From 1832 to 1834, one ran in Brussels. In 1834, a service was begun in Paris and over the next fifty years other services were established in France with several different types of steam vehicles.

But change was on the way. In 1860, the Frenchman Jean Lenoir built the first practical gas engine, and in 1863 tried it out on a vehicle. In 1864, Siegfried Marcus, an Austrian, built another vehicle driven by gasoline. But it was the invention, almost simultaneously, of gasoline engines by the Germans

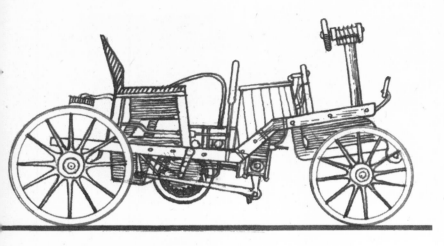
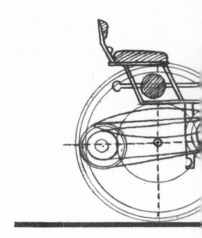

Gottlieb Daimler and Karl Benz, that really opened up new horizons for the automobile. Daimler patented his engine in 1885. In 1886, Benz put a gasoline-driven car on sale to the public for the first time. In 1891, the French carriage firm of Panhard and Levasser began using Daimler's engine to power the first Peugeots, and these cars were an immediate success.

Steam still had its disciples (steam cars were manufactured in America by the Stanley twins until the early 1920s), but its days were numbered. Steam cars were complicated, cumbersome, and, with their hissing boilers, potentially more dangerous.

In the late 1880s, electric cars became very popular. One built by Camille Jenatzy, a Belgian, reached the unheard-of speed of 65.79 mph in 1899. After the First World War, however, the electric car declined in popularity. Although it was quiet and did not give off offensive fumes, its batteries needed recharging about every 50 miles.

The general design of the automobile, and one which has persisted to the present day, was worked out by the French firm of Panhard and Levasser.

Amédée Bollée invented the gearbox in 1879, and this was adopted by Panhard in 1891. In 1895, de Dion-Bouton replaced the chain drive by a universal joint shaft. Another French manufacturer, Louis Renault, developed the direct shaft and applied it to his own models in 1898. In 1895, the Michelin brothers introduced pneumatic car tires.

Thanks to all these improvements, speed, power, and safety were steadily increasing. But the building of an automobile was still a craftsman's job, slow and expensive. The cheap car was yet to come.

The Industrial Era

The father of mass production was an American, Ransom E. Olds. In 1901, he introduced assembly-line methods. Car parts made by skilled workmen were assembled by semi-skilled men, each one attaching a particular part, as the car moved down the production line on a trolley. This made the cars much cheaper. In 1909, Henry Ford took the idea one stage further and decided to produce only one kind of car,

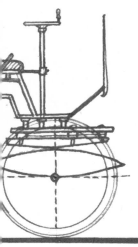

Far left: Motor vehicle built by engineer Sigfried Marcus in 1875; it is now in the Technische Museum, Vienna, Austria. Left: Gasoline-engined Victoria of Gottlieb Daimler, 1886; now in the Mercedes Museum, Stuttgart, Germany.

1

2

3

the Model T. In one year, he sold 19,000. In 1913, Ford fitted his production lines with conveyor belts instead of trolleys. This speeded things up even more. Within three years he was making nearly 750,000 cars a year, and the cheap car had really arrived.

World War I created a great demand for cars. The 700 Renault taxis of Paris were used for the first mass motorized transport of troops, carrying four thousand men to the battle of the Marne. Light vehicles were used for reconnaissance and liaison. Trucks became indispensable. During the terrible battle of Verdun, the rate of vehicles on the main road to the front was 6,000 in 24 hours—one every 14 seconds.

The car industry made a great contribution, too, to the production of munitions during the war. The young French industrialist André Citroën applied Ford's methods to the manufacture of shells, and after the war used

1. First Panhard-Levassor, front motor, 1893.
2. Small private bus of Amédée Bollée, Jr., 1901.
3. Stanley steam roadster, Stanley Brothers, 1910.
4. Tin Lizzie, Henry Ford's Model T, was first produced in 1909; the car shown here is the 1911 model.

4

On September 6th, 1914, 700 Renault taxis transported five battalions of France's 103rd and 104th infantry regiments (about 4,000 men) 31 miles from Gagny to Nanteuil-le-Haudouin. Each vehicle carried, besides the driver, five soldiers and traveled at an average speed of 19 mph. This was the famous episode of the Taxis of the Marne.

the same techniques to produce inexpensive cars. He had immediate success in 1919 with his 10-horsepower A type, which carried a family of four at a speed of more than 40 mph. Just as successful were the later models B2, B12, B14, and the famous two-seater of 1921, which was named the Ace of Clubs after the addition of a third seat.

In 1934, Citroën produced a revolutionary new car, the front-wheel drive C7. Everything about it was new—the body of chassisless single-shell construction, the independent suspension to all four wheels, and the engine. A remarkable road-holder and much ahead of its time, the C7 was produced for twenty

years with little variation in its design.

In the United States, Ford, having exhausted the success of the Model T, popularized the V8 engine invented by de Dion at the beginning of the century, and Chrysler paved the way to aerodynamic bodywork with the Airflow.

In 1939, war came again to Europe. While occupied countries had to go back to old types of transport—electric, gas, and gasogene motors—British, and later American, industry was organizing a gigantic production of trucks, light cars, armored cars, amphibious vehicles, and tanks with which to take the fight back to the Germans.

After the war, economic conditions in Europe greatly influenced car design. Shortage of gasoline, and heavy taxes on cars, among other things, made the manufacturers turn to the production of small cars that were cheap to make and to run. The large output called for required huge industrial plants, using all the new techniques of automation. Only the very largest manufacturers had the resources to carry out such extensive refitting programs in their factories.

Before the war, the Germans had planned the Volkswagen (the "people's car"), but only when peace was restored could it be manufactured in quantity. Other popular small cars are the Simca 1000 and the R-8 in France, the NSU Prinz 4 in Germany, and the Austin Mini, the Morris Minor, and the Hillman Imp in Britain.

So that small cars could carry more passengers, some of them had all the moving mechanical parts mounted at one end so that the transmission shaft did not pass through the inside. Everything was mounted in the rear in cars such as the VW, R-8, Simca 1000, and NSU, and in the front in cars such as the B.M.C. Austin Mini, R-4, and Panhard. Sometimes the engine is mounted sideways, too, as in the Austin Mini, the Simca 100, and the Peugeot 204.

The small family cars of today can travel quite fast. Some average maxi-

The Renault FT 17, the prototype of which was tried out in April, 1917. Twenty-one of these tanks appeared in combat in May, 1918, at Chaudun. Nicknamed the Victory Tank, weighing 7 tons, and carrying two men, it was armed with a machine gun (front tank) or a 37 mm cannon (rear tank).

mum speeds are: Renault Dauphine, 82 mph; Hillman Imp, 80 mph; Austin Mini, 74 mph; Simca 1000, 80 mph; Ford Anglia, 75 mph; Morris Minor 1000, 77 mph; Morris 1100, 76 mph. Average top speeds for some of the bigger and more expensive cars are: Chrysler New Yorker, Cadillac Fleetwood, Rolls-Royce Silver Shadow, Bentley Series T Saloon, all 120 mph. Sports cars, of course, are the fastest of all on the roads. Some average maximum speeds are Jensen C-V8 Mk III, 138 mph; Bristol 409 Saloon, 132 mph; Jaguar-E-Type, 150 mph; Maserati Mistrale, 155 mph; Aston Martin DB6, 150 mph. Larger family cars have speeds of: Austin A60 Cambridge, 84 mph; Volvo 122 S, 98 mph; Rover 2000, 104 mph; Vauxhall Victor, 85 mph.

In the United States, cheap gasoline and an enormous network of wide roads favored the building of high pow-

1. Front wheel drive Citroën, 1934, the first European aerodynamic car, without a chassis, of single-shell construction.
2. Chrysler Airflow, 1934, first aerodynamic production car in the United States.
Three postwar cars:
3. Volkswagon, 1953.
4. Austin Cooper, 1968.
5. Ford Mustang, 1968.

Two prestige cars, popular between the wars:
Duesenberg S J, 1935; 320 horsepower; eight
in-line cylinders; short chassis; maximum speed,
130 mph.

Hispano-Suiza, 1927; 6 cylinder motor, 150 horsepower.

ered cars. Because the V8 engine was
the most widely used, it has become
the most popular engine in the world.

Americans, however, were amazed
by the performances of small European
cars and imported them in large quantities, the Volkswagen and Dauphine in
particular. But their own manufacturers
countered this by producing so-called
"compact" cars—small for America, but
similar in size to large European cars.
One of these compact cars, the Chevro-
let Corvair, has in its turn had a great

influence on the shape of certain European vehicles such as the Fiat 1500 and
also the NSU Prinz.

American manufacturers also developed automatic transmission, a system
which relieves the driver of the bother
of shifting gears. This system is being
adopted by many European car manufacturers, even on small models. The
little Dutch Daf, a two-door sedan of
only 746 cc capacity, has belt-drive
automatic transmission.

Expensive "prestige" cars can be

Mercedes-Benz pullman, 1961; 300 horsepower V8 engine, top speed of 118 mph.

bought, naturally, by only the wealthiest people. Acknowledged as the best car in the world is the Rolls-Royce Silver Shadow, which blends the traditional craftsmanship of Rolls-Royce with modern body styling. It seats five and has an engine of V8-cylinder, 6,230 cc capacity. The most luxurious car made by B.M.C. is the Vanden Plas Princess 4-Litre, often used on state and ceremonial occasions because of its dignified appearance. With an average maximum speed of 93 mph, it seats from 6 to 8 and has a 6-cylinder engine of 3,993 cc capacity. Other cars in this luxury class are the Mercedes 600, the Cadillac, and the Chrysler Imperial.

The Car of Tomorrow

The car of tomorrow is beginning to take shape. The once enormous engine is getting smaller and smaller. The flat Volkswagen 1500 engine takes up the minimum of space at the back of the car, and the even smaller rotary Wankel engine produced by NSU is certain to come into commercial use. Chrysler has already fitted some of its cars with turbine engines. Remarkable for its smooth and quiet running, the turbine will no doubt be adopted more widely when problems of noise and fuel consumption have been overcome. Controls developed by Turbomeca for the French aircraft industry might well mean that the driving of a turbine car will not differ greatly from conventional driving. The Rover-B.R.M. turbine racing car, as we shall see a little later on, gave a very good account of itself in the 24-hour race at Le Mans.

Streamlined body of a car of tomorrow, the GM-X of General Motors. The bodywork in plastic is inspired by aerodynamic shapes.

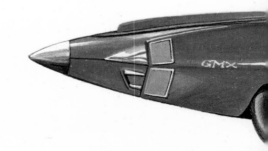

Races and Rallies

Apart from the thrills it gives to millions of spectators, racing provides a lot of the information essential to the development of the automobile. From the performance of the car at top speed under grueling conditions, manufacturers can discover which particular pieces of equipment can be improved or redesigned to make the vehicle faster and safer. Many of these improvements are then used on ordinary production models for the family motorist.

Automobile racing began in France. The world's first "automobile trial," which is a form of race, took place on a 20-mile course from Paris to Versailles and back in 1887. It was won by Georges Bouton's steam quadricycle at an average speed of 16 mph. In 1895, the Paris-Bordeaux-Paris race was won by a Panhard-Levasser, with a Daimler engine, at an average speed of 15 mph. In 1899, the first Tour de France, over 1,255 miles, was won by a Panhard at nearly 30 mph. In 1901, a Mors was the winner of the Paris-Bordeaux race at almost 50 mph. The Paris-Berlin and Paris-Vienna races were again French victories. The first day's run of the Paris-Madrid race in 1903 was won at an average speed of more than 65 mph. But three drivers, among them Marcel Renault, brother of the manufacturer, were killed on the first day, and the French Government stopped the race at Bordeaux. From then on, races were held on closed circuits, and special tracks were built. The Gordon-Bennett Cup (1900-1905), the Grand Prix of the Automobile Club of France (1906), and the Vanderbilt Cup (1905) in the United States were the world's first "classic" races. The French Grand Prix is still being run, the second oldest auto race in the world. The oldest is the R.A.C. Tourist Trophy, first held on the Isle of Man in 1905.

After the speed races came the en-

The first automobile trial was held in 1887. Another early motor race was the one from Paris to Rouen in 1894. It was won by the Marquis de Dion on his steam tractor; this vehicle was designed to pull a four-wheeled carriage at a speed of 9 mph.

In 1907, the British racing track at Brooklands was built. In 1909, the Indianapolis track was opened in the United States. The dangerous Indianapolis 500-mile race was held there for the first time in 1911. Up to 1968, in 52 races, 54 drivers had been killed in this event. The record time for the 500 miles is the 3 hours 16 minutes 13.76 seconds set up in 1968 by the American driver Bobby Unser in a 2.75-liter 625 brake horsepower Eagle-Offenhauser Rislone Special—an average speed of 152.88 mph. It was not until 1924 that France, the pioneer of auto racing, had its own big track at Linas-Montlhéry.

durance runs. In 1903 Tom Fetch crossed the United States from San Francisco to New York in 61 days in the Packard, Old Pacific. In 1907, the Peking-Paris race of 7,500 miles was won in 60 days by Prince Scipione Borghesi in an Itala.

Between the two world wars, the usual victors on the tracks were Delage, Bugatti, Alfa Romeo, Mercedes, and Auto-Union. Since 1950, the first places have been taken by Maserati, Ferrari, Mercedes, Cooper, B.R.M., and Lotus. Their latest cars have all adopted John Cooper's idea of putting the engine at the rear and having the driver lie almost flat on his back in a low-slung, streamlined cockpit.

The 24-hour Grand Prix d'Endurance at Le Mans, France, is the world's most

Paris-Madrid in 1903. In the lead a Clement, and behind it the Mors driven by Gabriel, winner of the Paris-Bordeaux lap. Because of fatal accidents, the race was stopped at Bordeaux.

The famous Old 16, victor of the Vanderbilt cup in the United States in 1908. During the Gordon-Bennett cup on the Auvergne circuit in 1905, a vehicle of this type, driven by Tracy, had to be abandoned at the second lap.

important sports car race, held on a circuit of 8.36 miles. The first, held in 1923, was won by a 3-liter Chenard et Walcker, which covered 1,367 miles at an average speed of more than 57 mph. In 1967, A. J. Foyt, Jr. and Daniel Gurney, both of the United States, covered the greatest-ever distance, 3,251.57 miles, at an average speed of 135.48 mph. In 1963, the Rover-B.R.M. turbine car took part for the first time and averaged 108 mph. The lap record for the circuit is 3 minutes 23.6 seconds, an average speed of 147.89 mph, set up by Denis Hulme of the United States in a 7-liter Ford. Records do not stand for long, however. They are broken every year.

Because of the difference in size and performance of racing cars, the Inter-national Automobile Federation has laid down formulas, or classifications, for race entrants. The formulas are revised, if need be, every three years.

Formula One

One-seater cars of 3,000 cc maximum capacity unsupercharged, or 1,500 cc supercharged.

Formula Two

One-seaters with four-cylinder motors and a maximum capacity of 1,500 cc.

Formula Three

One-seaters of 1,000 cc, whose parts must come from cars in ordinary production. (This allows young drivers to race at a reasonable cost.)

Formula Four

One-seaters of up to 250 cc, no more than two cylinders, and the engine to cost not more than $420. Total weight not to exceed 500 pounds.

There are many rallies in which sports cars or grand touring (GT) cars can compete according to their engine capacity. The two greatest road rallies are the Monte Carlo Rally and the Tour de France Automobile. The Monte Carlo Rally, first held in 1911, is competed in by cars that are especially improved and equipped for the run and are driven by the most experienced rally drivers. The Tour de France accepts any car, from the ordinary sports car to the most powerful GT.

In rallies, as in track racing, equipment is tested on sports or GT cars before being applied on production models. Racing benefits the motor industry in another way, too; victory in a race increases the sales and exports of similar models and encourages other manufacturers to improve their own cars in the hope of catching up.

The Highest Speed on Wheels

The first true speed record was established in 1898, when a Frenchman, Gaston Chasseloup-Laubat, drove at 39.24 mph in an electric Jeantaud. In April, 1899, Camille Jenatzy, a Belgian, reached a speed of 65.79 mph in the electric *Jamais Contente*. Leon Serpollet, in a steam car of his own design,

Graham Hill at the wheel of a Lotus Ford Formula 1 Grand Prix car. This car is powered by a Ford Cosworth V8 engine.

Ford MK II, powered by a 7,000 cc engine developing 500 horsepower.

held the record for four months in 1902 with a speed of 75.06 mph. But the gasoline-driven car was catching up. In August, 1902, William K. Vanderbilt, Jr. reached 76.08 mph in a Mors. In 1904, Henry Ford became the first man to travel officially at 100 mph. Steam came back into the lead in 1906 when the Stanley Steamer, driven by the American Frank H. Marriott, did 127.-57 mph. Early the next year, Marriott was said to have done another run at 180 mph; on his second run over the mile, he was nearing 197 mph when his car overturned into the sea.

Between World War I and World War II, two great English drivers battled for the title of the fastest man in the world—Sir Henry Seagrave and Sir Malcolm Campbell. Seagrave in 1927 reached 207.02 mph in a Sunbeam. Campbell, in Bluebird I, a special car of his own design powered by a Napier engine, reached 214.80 mph in 1928. In his Golden Arrow, also with a Napier engine, Seagrave regained his title the following year with 233.01 mph. Camp-

bell took up the challenge again, and in 1931, at the wheel of Bluebird II, he reached 246.63 mph. By 1935, this time with Bluebird III, powered by a Rolls-Royce engine, Malcolm Campbell was able to travel at 304.31 mph.

A new fight for first place opened later between two other Englishmen—George Eyston and John Cobb. In 1937 and 1938, Eyston nudged up his speed from 319.11 mph to 347.49 mph. Cobb took the record from him on September 15th, 1938, at 353.29 mph, but Eyston was back, the very next day, with a speed of 359.64 mph. Just before the outbreak of war in 1939, Cobb was again world champion with 371.58 mph, and after the war, in 1947, pushed it up to 394.2 mph.

In November, 1965, Bob Summers, on the Bonneville Salt Flats in Utah, beat the record for a vehicle with conventional propulsion. He made 407 mph in Goldenrod, a car fitted with four Chrysler V8 engines. This beat the previous record set up by the late Donald Campbell, Sir Malcolm's son,

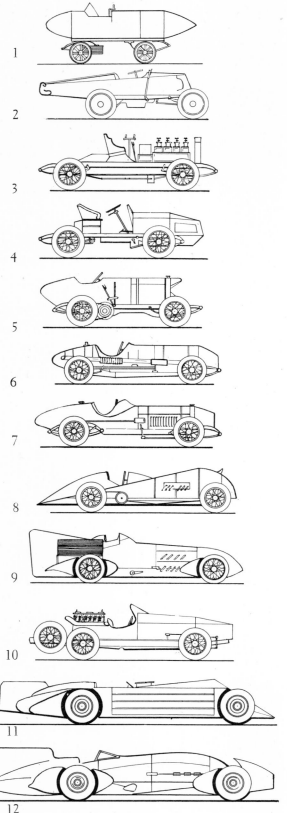

Highest speeds on wheels, 1899 to 1965, including car, driver; place, date; and mph.

1. Jamais Contente, Jenatzy; Achère, Belgium, 1899; 65.79 mph.
2. Serpollet, Serpollet; Nice, France, 1902; 75.06 mph.
3. Ford 999, Oldfield; St. Clair Lake, Michigan, 1903; 91 mph.
4. Darracq, Baras; Montgeron, France, 1904; 104 mph.
5. Blitzen Benz, Oldfield; Daytona Beach, Florida, 1910; 132.05 mph.
6. Sunbeam, K.L. Guinness; Brooklands, England, 1922; 133 mph.
7. Delage, René Thomas; Arpajon, France; 143 mph.
8. Thomas Special, J.G. Parry-Thomas; Pendine Sands, England, 1926; 170.8 mph.
9. Bluebird I (Napier-Campbell), Malcolm Campbell; Daytona Beach, Florida, 1928; 214.80 mph.
10. White Triplex, Ray Keech; Daytona Beach, Florida, 1928; 207.5 mph.
11. Golden Arrow (Irving-Napier), H. Seagrave; Daytona Beach, Florida, 1929, 233.01 mph.
12. Bluebird II (Napier-Campbell), Sir Malcolm Campbell; Daytona Beach, Florida, 1931; 246.63 mph.
13. Bluebird III, Sir Malcolm Campbell; Bonneville, Utah, 1935; 304.311 mph.
14. Thunderbolt, G.E.T. Eyston; Bonneville, Utah, 1938; 359.636 mph.
15. Railton-Mobil, John Cobb; Bonneville, Utah, 1947; 394.2 mph.
16. Bluebird (gas turbine), Donald Campbell; Lake Eyre, Australia, 1964; 403.1 mph.
17. Green Monster (power jet), Art Arfons; Bonneville, Utah, 1965; 576.6 mph.

Spirit of America. In November, 1965, Craig Breedlove reached the speed of 554.28 mph in his new racer. Art Arfons, driving his Green Monster, bettered this record with a speed of 576.6 mph. Eight days later, Breedlove made a try to break the Arfons record and succeeded with a speed of 599.48 mph. His record is so far unbeaten.

in July, 1964. Driving Bluebird, which was powered by a gas turbine engine, Campbell's average time for two runs had been 403.1 mph.

These speeds for conventionally propelled cars, however, are left far behind by those reached by jet-propelled vehicles which, since 1963, have been allowed to compete. Each year American drivers Craig Breedlove and Art Arfons battle it out in their jet-powered machines. Breedlove, in his Spirit of America, scored first in 1963 with a speed of 436.60 mph. Arfons, in Green Monster,

replied in October, 1964, with 491.90 mph. Back came Breedlove that same month to break the record three times with speeds of 507.47 mph, 519.49 mph, and 547.42 mph. But the final 1964 victory went to Arfons with a speed of 571.38 mph. In 1965, Art Arfons reached 576.6 mph, but Craig Breedlove overtook him with an average for the mile of 600.6 mph. And in the same year, Craig Breedlove broke his own record with a speed of 613.99 mph over 666 yards in the Spirit of America-Sonic I.

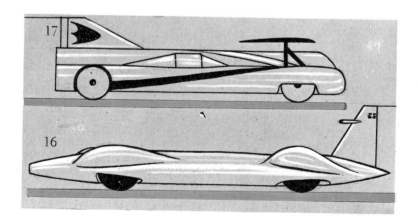

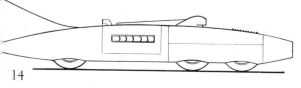

14

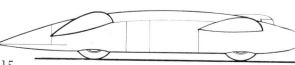

15

Speed
on Rails

Partnership of Rail and
Steam Power

In the 19th century, the riches of the Western world began to increase at a rate never before dreamed of. This was due to a great extent to the introduction of machinery and methods that made the production of things like cloth, coal, and iron much faster, easier, and cheaper. It was due also to a partnership that made it possible for goods and people to be carried at greatly increased speeds—the partnership of the rail and the steam-powered engine.

In ancient Greece and Rome, double tracks of stone or wood were laid in wagon ruts to keep carts and chariots from being bogged down in wet weather. In the 16th century, miners in Europe laid down wooden rails, along which they pushed their trucks of coal and metal ore. In English mines in the 18th century, the wooden tracks were covered with iron plates. In 1768, cast iron rails replaced wooden ones for good. By this time, the rail had long proved its worth. The reduction in friction on the wheels meant that a horse or a man could move a much greater weight with the same effort.

These first iron rails, called plateways, had flanges on the inside edges to keep the wheels from slipping off the track. In 1789, the Englishman Jessop invented the rail as we know it today. The flange was taken off the rail, leaving it simply a metal strip called an edge rail, and the flange was put on the wheel.

Horse-drawn railway wagons were in common use in mines and quarries from the late 1600s. In 1803, the world's first public goods line, the Surrey Iron Railway, was opened in Britain. The following year, Richard Trevithick showed that steam power could replace

Race between Peter Cooper's steam locomotive, *Tom Thumb*, and a horse-drawn train, in February, 1827, in the United States. The locomotive was beaten by the horse.

George Stephenson's *Rocket.* In Lancashire, England, it won first place in the locomotive race in 1829; it ran the last mile at more than 30 mph.

the horse. His engine, the first rail-borne locomotive in history, successfully hauled a train loaded with ten tons of iron ore and 70 passengers in South Wales. It was hardly a fast run —the train drew its load at 5 mph and had a top speed of only 15 mph. But Trevithick had started something. The great partnership had begun.

Trevithick's engine, however, was not a complete success. It was too heavy for the cast iron tracks of the day. Trevithick went to London to open a circle of track on which the public was invited to take shilling rides as a novelty, but the engine was derailed and the track

closed down. Engineers, believing that wheels would slip on smooth rails, turned their attention to experiments with toothed rails. All sorts of designs were produced, incorporating ridges, claws, props, and winches, and the advance of the railway slowed down for several years until 1813, when Christopher Blackett built his *Puffing Billy* for the Wylam Colliery in Northumberland, England.

In 1814, a young British engineer named George Stephenson demonstrated his first locomotive. It was the first smooth-wheeled locomotive to run on edge rails, and a great success, but Stephenson was not satisfied. The old cast iron rails, he decided, were not strong enough. If the locomotives were to have any future, the rails must be of wrought iron.

Stephenson's great opportunity came when he was given the task of building a twelve-mile railway from the mining town of Darlington to the shipping town of Stockton. On September 27th, 1825, the Stockton and Darlington Railway was opened, with Stephenson at the controls of his *Locomotion No. 1,*

The General was a locomotive typical of those used on the early railroads in the American West.

Right: *Puffing Billy* was in use on British railways for more than 50 years, from 1813 to 1864. It weighed 8 tons and could haul 50 tons at 5 mph.

Locomotive designed by Robert Stephenson, 1864. The majority of early English railways were attributed to this inventor.

The Empire State Express, New York, at the turn of the century.

pulling 34 wagons carrying goods and 600 passengers. The railway had begun.

Railway enthusiasts still argue about which was the first real railway as we know it, the Stockton and Darlington or the Liverpool and Manchester, opened in 1830. Some of the Stockton trains were still drawn by horses, but the Liverpool and Manchester trains were all steam-hauled.

Stephenson, helped by his son, Robert, built the Liverpool and Manchester line. They also built the engine that won the competition held to choose the locomotives for the run. That engine was the *Rocket*, the most famous locomotive ever built. The contest was held in 1829 in Lancashire, and five engines were entered—the *Cycloped, Perseverance, Novelty, Sans Pareil,* and the *Rocket*. Each had to weigh no more than six tons, and to pull without stopping a train three times its own weight at a speed of 10 mph on the level.

Cycloped and *Perseverance* were soon eliminated. *Sans Pareil* was too clumsy to stay long in the running. *Novelty* got off to a wonderful start, but could not sustain the power and kept having to stop. The *Rocket,* presented by Robert Stephenson, with his

The locomotive *Mountain*, first of this type in Europe, ran in 1925.

49

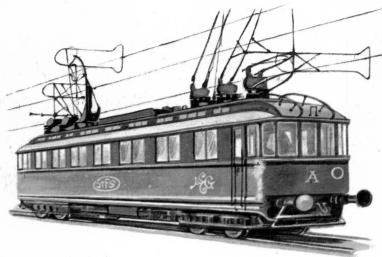

First electric traction. The German railcar of Siemens und Halske, driven by three-phase current, reached 130.61 mph in 1903.

father at the controls, sped up and down the track over and over again. When the wagons and tender were taken off, it reached more than 30 mph. The result was decisive, and the railway at once ordered eight more locomotives like it.

From then onward, railways spread rapidly, both in Britain and overseas. The first in France was opened in 1837. In the United States, the Baltimore and Ohio Railroad was opened in 1830 with 13 miles of track. By 1860 the United States had 30,000 miles of railroads. Between 1835 and 1840, Belgium, Germany, Russia, Holland, and Austria all began building their own networks.

Speeds began to increase as more advanced locomotives took to the rails. In 1839, in Staffordshire, England, a Grand Junction Railway engine reached 56.75 mph. In 1848, the Great Western

Union Pacific steam locomotive *Big Boy*. This locomotive was the longest and heaviest ever built.

Railway engine *Great Britain* reached 78 mph. In 1893, speeds of 102.8 mph and 112.5 mph were claimed for two American trains, but these are not generally regarded as authentic.

Speeds over long distances were improving, too. In 1899, the *China and Japan Mail* crossed the North American continent from Vancouver to New York (3,107 miles) at an average speed of more than 37 mph, including stops. At the same time the speed of the expresses from Paris to Marseilles was 41.5 mph. Between Jersey City and Washington, D.C., the *Royal Blue Limited* covered 225 miles in 4.5 hours without stops, an average of nearly 50 mph. The Berlin-Hamburg train traveled the 178 miles at an average speed of 51 mph, and the *Empire State Express* ran from New York City to Buffalo, 435 miles, carrying 250 tons, at 53.5 mph.

The 100-mph train was becoming a possibility by the end of the 19th century. In 1897, an English Midland Railway locomotive traveled at 90 mph.

First diesel-electric express train. The *Flying Hamburger* was introduced into service in 1933 on the Berlin-Hamburg line.

But by this time a rival had appeared —the electric locomotive.

Steam v. Electricity

The railroads' conquest of time and distance was not made by steam alone. Quite early, electricity began to take over. Steam, which gave the railways their early character and excitement, has now to a large extent disappeared as the old locomotives are replaced by electric or diesel engines.

We have seen that, in 1897, a steam train reached 90 mph. The distinction

Turbo-electric locomotive put into service in 1960 in the United States. A gas turbine powers the generators, which provide the electric current for the motors; maximum speed 65 mph.

of being the first train to travel at 100 mph, however, went to the *Siemens und Halske Electric* which, in 1901, traveled at 101 mph near Berlin, Germany. In 1903, *Siemens und Halske* broke the record three times, with speeds of 124.89 mph, 128.43 mph, and 130.61 mph. And this was in 1903!

For its size, an electric locomotive can produce much more power than a steam locomotive. To build a steam engine with the same power as a really fast electric engine would mean building a monstrously big machine, which would create problems of track-holding and braking power.

A locomotive or wagon on rails has movements that affect its track-holding —rolling, galloping (a movement like the pitching of a ship), swaying (shaking from one rail to the other), vertical parallel oscillations, and horizontal parallel oscillations. These and other problems, such as the taking of bends, skidding, and balance of suspension,

have all had to be tackled by engineers to produce the safe trains of today.

Today, most trains are fitted with compressed air brakes, and research is constantly going on to make them function even better than they do now. Stopping a train at high speed poses tremendous problems. You have only to imagine what happens on the rail when a steel wheel suddenly stops turning, to realize what the difficulties are. The train driver must keep in mind when he applies the brakes such facts as the degree of friction for a steel tire against a rail, which varies according to whether the day is damp or dry. He must also remember not to lock the wheels completely at the moment of braking. This not only creates less friction and starts a skid, but it results in greater wear on the wheels.

With a compressed air system, using conventional brake shoes, it is possible to stop a train moving at over 74 mph within 601 yards; at 87 mph within

820 yards. Trials are going on in the United States of brakes that will stop a train moving at 99.5 mph within 1,203 yards. Above 112 mph, other braking systems have to be used—electromagnetic, propeller, or even jet turbine.

Electricity has triumphed over steam simply because it does the job better in so many ways. Its advantages are fuel efficiency (there is little loss of energy in comparison with steam), flexibility of use, greater acceleration, ease of maintenance, speed of starting, and the possibility of crew changes at any time (steam trains need crews familiar with the particular type). Electricity makes great speeds possible over short as well as long distances. The variable torque of an electric locomotive gives extremely fast acceleration. Even on a run of less than four miles, speeds of over 80 mph can be reached; this is impossible with a steam engine over such a short distance.

Since the first electric line was built in Berlin in 1879, electric trains have never stopped improving in performance. Speeds of 100 mph are now commonplace. The 212 miles between Tokyo and Nagoya in Japan are covered in 2 hours at an average speed of 106 mph, the world's fastest regular run. Travelers in Italy can get from Rome to Milan in six hours. The distance is 394 miles. This may seem to be not so great a distance to cover in the time, but the route is a winding one over some very mountainous country. In Britain, electric trains run the 100 miles between London and Birmingham in 95 minutes, including stops. The French train 320 travels the 41 miles from Arras to Longueau in 29 minutes, an average speed of 84.8 mph. The fastest time made by a steam train was 126 mph reached in 1938 by the *Mallard*, drawing seven cars weighing 240 tons. The fastest trains in the world are two French electric locomotives, the *CC7107* and the *BB9004*. In 1955, each reached a speed of 205.6 mph, drawing three cars weighing 100 tons.

The diesel engine is another form of locomotion which has helped to push steam out of favor. Diesel locomotives can be diesel-mechanical, diesel-hydraulic, or diesel-electric, according to the way in which the power is transmitted to the wheels. Diesel-hydraulic transmission is made through an oil-filled gear box known as a hydraulic torque converter. Diesel-electric transmission uses the diesel engine to turn electric generators which supply power to the traction motors. Diesel-mechanical transmission is through a clutch plate like that of an automobile. This is not really satisfactory for heavy railroad work so, if it is used at all, it is usually combined with the hydraulic system.

Penn Central's *Metroliner*. In this new high-speed train, trips between Washington, D.C., and New York take only 2 hours 59 minutes.

Diesel trains were adopted by many countries, particularly the United States, after they proved successful in Germany. The diesel's suitability for long hauls has led to its almost exclusive use in North America. In Britain a large "dieselization" program has resulted in their extensive use. The English *Deltic* diesel-electric locomotives can travel at more than 100 mph, pulling 500-ton expresses between London and Edinburgh, Scotland. The first diesel express was the German train *The Flying Hamburger*, which in 1933 reached speeds of 117 mph. Diesels can pull great loads at an average speed of 90 mph with no trouble at all and have, like electric locomotives, much faster acceleration than steam engines. They are cheaper to run and to service, can make long runs without refueling, and have the further advantage that the track does not have to be changed for them, as it does for electric trains.

The passenger train of the future may well be the monorail, powered by electricity, gas, gasoline, or even rockets. The monorail, as its name implies, has only one rail. Cars run either above or below it. Those that run above it are balanced either by the use of gripping wheels or gyroscopic devices. The monorail has the great advantage of not using up valuable land for tracks. Mounted on pillars, the rails run high above the ground, leaving the area under them free for other uses.

The word monorail sounds as modern as tomorrow, but the world's first was built in 1824! Its cars were drawn by horses, and it was built at the London docks by Henry Palmer, an engineer who built another one in 1825 to carry bricks over marshland.

A monorail car produced in 1897 reached a speed of 83 mph. A monorail railroad built by a Spaniard, Lartigue, was in operation in Ireland from 1888 to 1924. The oldest monorail still in service is an eight-mile system in Germany, built in 1901. The top speed is only 23 mph, but because there are 18 stations on the track, a higher speed would not be possible over such short distances. In the United States in 1910, a 1.5-mile track was built, on top of which an electric car ran at 60 mph. The track, however, had not been built strongly enough, and one day the car came off because it went around a curve too *slowly*. This sounds strange, but the reason was that there was not enough centrifugal force to counteract the full weight of the car at low speed. The United States did not get its second monorail until 1956, when the *Skyway* system was built at Houston, Texas. In Japan an 8.5-mile length of rail links the center of Tokyo with the city's airport. The highest speed attained on a suspended monorail is 235 mph, achieved in 1967 by the experimental rocket-boosted, jet-powered *L'Aerotrain* invented by Jean Bertin.

A British invention for use in deserts, the *George Bennie Airspeed Railway*, has cars powered by propellers; they can reach 150 mph in a quarter of a mile. This is not, strictly speaking, a monorail, because it has a second rail underneath the car to prevent swaying.

A glimpse of what might be in store for future monorail travelers can be had from the results of tests with a rocket-powered sled on the 6.62-mile track at a U.S. Air Force missile experimental station in New Mexico. Carrying a chimpanzee, the sled touched 1,295 mph. Empty, it reached 3,090 mph, the highest speed ever reached on rails.

CHAPTER FIVE

Speed on Water

The First Boats

Man learned to ride on water in the same way as many another creature before him—by falling in and grabbing at a passing log or branch. In time, he conquered his fear and began to take to the water deliberately, sitting astride a log and paddling with his hands, finding it easier, faster, and safer than pushing his way overland through mountain and jungle.

Later still he learned to tie together bundles of reeds or branches to make rafts, to hollow out logs with fire and stone axes, and still later to make paddles, oars, and sails. The process continued with the inventions of the machine age—steam engines, paddle wheels, propellers, steam turbines, gasoline and diesel engines all helped to make ships bigger and faster. It goes on still. The nuclear-powered ship has been a reality since 1954, and in years to come probably all the bigger ships will be driven by atomic reactors.

Water covers seven tenths of the earth's surface, separating the lands and peoples of the world by thousands of miles of trackless ocean. For this reason, if for no other, it is hardly surprising that man has spent much time, effort, and money on building and improving his ships, turning the seas and rivers into highways, instead of leaving them as barriers.

Communications on the ocean shipping routes were speeded up by the opening in 1869 of the Suez Canal, which connects the Mediterranean and the Red Sea, and the opening in 1914 of the Panama Canal, which connects the Atlantic and the Pacific.

Navigation in Ancient Times

At first, speed on water was not important. The big problem was to build boats that would stay afloat. Many primitive types of boats that proved their water-worthiness are still in use

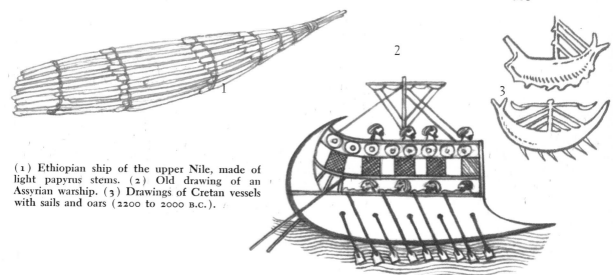

(1) Ethiopian ship of the upper Nile, made of light papyrus stems. (2) Old drawing of an Assyrian warship. (3) Drawings of Cretan vessels with sails and oars (2200 to 2000 B.C.).

today—dug-out canoes, log rafts, catamarans, canoes made from bundles of papyrus reeds, and coracles made by covering a wickerwork frame with animal skins or tarred canvas.

There was a limit, however, to the loads these crude boats could carry, and a limit to their range, too. The first sizable seagoing craft were built in the lands around the Mediterranean, whose calm and tideless waters were ideal for sea trading. The first known reference to a sail is on an 8,000-year-old Egyptian pot. The Egyptians, the Cretans, the Phoenicians, and the Greeks all put to sea many hundreds of years before Christ to trade and fight in ships powered by sail and oar. The

Phoenicians were the most enterprising of these ancient traders, sailing as far north as Britain and as far south as East Africa. They realized the value of speed in commerce and used oar and sail on their merchant ships. Mainly, however, the early trading ships relied on sail. Oars were used, often in several banks, to give speed and maneuverability to the slim warships of the Mediterranean. Greed and envy soon caused wars and piracy on the sea, and the contrast between the slow, clumsy merchant ship and the sleek, fast ship of war is one that persists to this day.

Trade and war together, then as now, made men strive constantly to improve their vessels and led to the evolution of custom-built ships—ships designed especially for a particular purpose. The basic lesson of warfare was that a small, fast craft could overcome much bigger vessels simply by being able to dart in, damage its op-

Egyptian vessel of about 3000 B.C. with oars and sail.

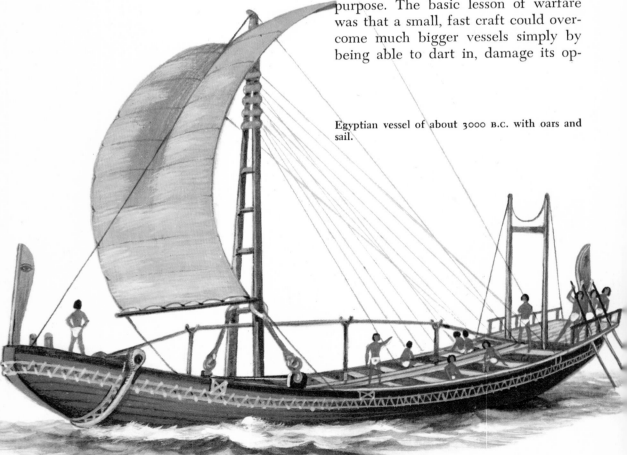

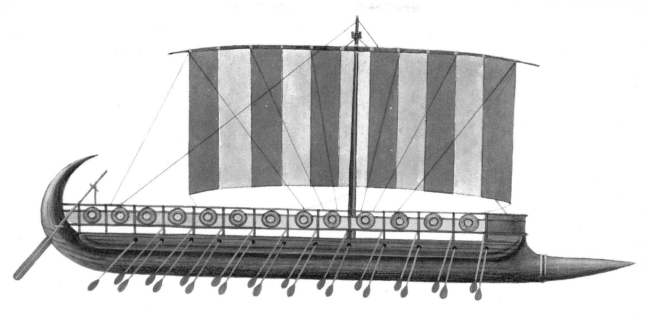

Ancient Phoenician Bireme with auxiliary sail, drawn after Assyrian reliefs. Note the ram on the bow and shields protecting the vessel's rowers.

ponent, and dart away again before it could be damaged itself. This happened in 480 B.C. when victory at Salamis went to the Greek galleys that outmaneuvered the large ships of Xerxes. It happened again, in 31 B.C. at Actium, when the galleys of Mark Antony and Cleopatra were put to flight by the lighter ships of Octavius.

The Romans achieved speed in spite of size in their large war galleys by equipping them with many oars. The Roman trireme of 400 B.C. was 140 feet long and carried three banks of oars on each side. So when a Roman galley went into action, there were as many as 120 men straining every muscle to send it where it was wanted.

From the Vikings to the Middle Ages

The progress of ship design, like most other progress, suffered a setback in the Western world when the Roman Empire collapsed under the onslaught of the barbarian tribes. But, as somewhat of a compensation for this, out

of the far north came a ship that was in many ways superior to the Mediterranean craft—the Viking longship. Sturdy enough to weather the Atlantic storms, powered by a single square sail and 40 or 50 brawny oarsmen, these ships struck terror into coast-dwellers of the north whenever they appeared over the horizon. For three hundred years, from the 8th to the 10th century, the Vikings harassed almost every country in Europe. They sailed down rivers into the heart of Russia (which is said to be named after a Viking tribe called the *Rus*), colonized Iceland and Greenland, and even discovered America five hundred years before Columbus. The Vikings were not simply pirates; above all they were farmers and traders. And they used not only their longships but shorter, rounder vessels for carrying goods, animals, and families to settle in their newly conquered lands.

From the 13th to the 15th century, ship design appeared to advance very little, although there were one or two small changes that were to be of im-

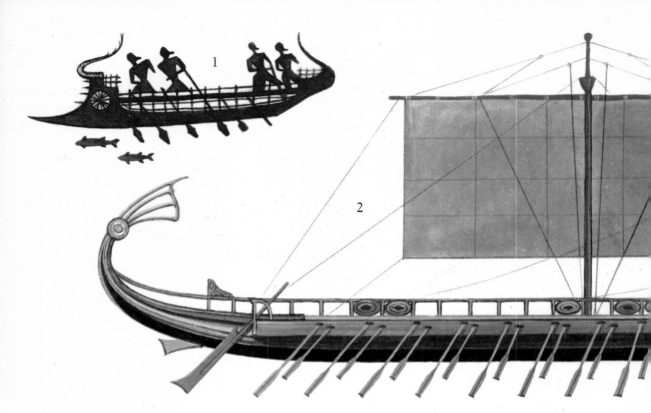

portance later on. The square sail had disappeared from the Mediterranean, replaced by the triangular lateen sail that the Arabs used on their dhows. With a lateen, a ship can sail more easily in light winds, so in the 15th and 16th centuries, European ships began to carry a lateen as well as a square sail to help in steering. Up until then, ships had been single-masted. Now a second mast, the mizzenmast behind the main-

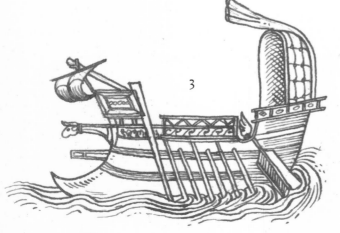

mast, was added to carry the lateen. A third mast, the foremast, was added later to carry another square sail for extra power.

The stern rudder was not in common use until the end of the 14th century. Before then ships were steered by a steerboard on the right-hand side; from this we get the term starboard, or right.

Ships really began to improve with the voyages of discovery of men like Columbus, who reached the West Indies in 1492, Vasco da Gama, who sailed around Africa in 1496, and Magellan, whose fleet was the first to sail around the world in 1521. Their discoveries meant more trade, greater riches, more to spend on making ships faster and safer.

The Great Days of Sail

From the 16th to the early 19th century was the golden age of sail. Spain,

Holland, and Britain were constant rivals for the mastery of the seas in the 16th and 17th centuries, and each built ships with ever increasing spreads of sail. They were still not fast, not even by ancient standards. The Roman galley could reach a speed of 8 knots (a knot is a nautical mile—6,080 feet— per hour). But these galleys were too fragile to stand up to rough weather. So the speed of 5 or 6 knots of the average sailing ship of Drake's time was not at all bad, considering that the vessel carried cargo, guns, crew, and was built stoutly enough to cross the open sea.

In the 18th century, hulls became slimmer and sails became bigger and more numerous. Masts were often more than 160 feet tall. This cramming-on of sails reached its peak in the mid-19th century in the face of competition from the new steam-driven vessels. The British battleship *Temeraire*,

1. Doric warship, Greece, 3300 B.C., depicted on a vase.
2. Greek Bireme, about 480 B.C.; note the symbolic eye on the bow.
3. Roman galley with ram and sail on the bowsprit and small poop deck at rear.
4. Roman Trireme with rostrum and large, square spritsail; forecastle for attack and shields for defense.

4

1

2

3

4

5

6

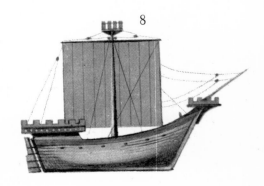

7

built in 1877, carried a mainsail of 5,100 square feet of canvas that weighed two tons. The ship's total sail area was 25,000 square feet. The mainmasts of three other ships built around that time measured 175 feet from top to bottom.

Even so, the 18th-century warship, because of the weight of its armament and the bulk needed to carry it, rarely exceeded 6 knots. It could be easily outsailed by the frigates, corvettes, and schooners of merchants, pirates, and slave traders. For a time, the slave ships were the fastest of all—not only to elude the pursuing warships, but to ensure that as little as possible of their miserable human cargo perished on a long journey.

The fastest and probably the most

8

1. Viking Drakkars (from the Bayeux tapestry) reached 165 or even 260 feet in length.
2, 3, 4, and 5. Silhouettes of Scandinavian barges.
6. English sailing ship with rudder and castles forward and aft; 13th century.
7. Baltic ship ornamented with animal heads; 13th century.
8. German Hanseatic Cog with lap-joints, fighting top, and castles forward and aft; 14th century.
9. Columbus's famous *Santa Maria*, 1492. A replica can be seen in Barcelona.
10. The English galleon *Henry Grâce à Dieu*, 1545, with six decks.

beautiful sailing ships ever built were the clippers. Developed by the Americans in the 1830's and 1840's, their design was taken up by the British in the 1860's. Used to carry tea from China and wood and gold from Australia, the fastest of the clippers could average 15 knots, and at times they reached a speed of more than 20 knots. Clippers like the American *Flying Cloud*, and the British *Thermopylae* and *Cutty Sark*, represented the peak of achievement in sail. The *Cutty Sark*, the most famous of them all, was built especially to outsail the *Thermopylae*, then the fastest ship of the day, on the run bringing tea from China. Once she covered 363 nautical miles in 24 hours, an average of more than 15 knots. Even this, however, did not match the achievement of the well named American *Sovereign of the Seas*, which in 1853 covered 410.7 nautical miles in 23 hours 18 minutes, an average of nearly 18 knots. Occasionally she reached 22 knots (25 mph).

Shipping company owners who preferred sailing ships to the new steamers made one last bid for survival with the windjammer. This was a slow, sturdy ship built of iron or steel, whose large holds could take 3,000 tons of cargo and whose design was such that it could sail safely through the roughest seas. In 1875, the first windjammer appeared. By the early 1900s, the last came into port for the last time. Steam had taken over the seas.

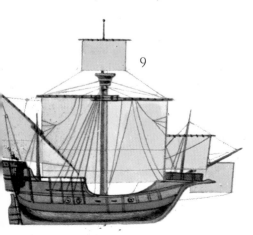

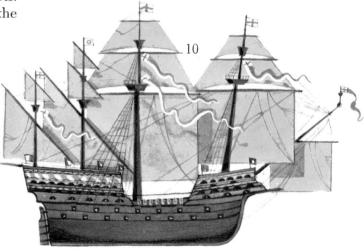

Three-decked vessel of the 18th century with three sets of square mainsails, which could carry studding sails, and bowsprit with jibs and spritsails. The frame of the poop was covered with lanterns and numerous sculptures.

Power-driven Ships

Toward the end of the 18th century, while the tall, proud sailing ships were crossing the seas of the world, several strange experimental vessels were chugging along rivers in France and the United States. Although they were regarded at first as curiosities, these "contraptions" were in time to doom the tall ships to an end in the breakers' yards.

In 1783, the Marquis d'Abbans made a trip on the River Seine in a steam-powered boat. The trip lasted only 15 minutes, but it was long enough to prove that steam propulsion on water was possible. In 1787, a craft designed by James Rumsey was tried out on the Potomac River in the United States. Driven by a water pump that used the jet principle, the craft reached 4 mph.

In 1802 came the first paddle steamer actually to be put to work. The *Char-lotte Dundas*, built by William Symington, and using an engine built by James Watt, hauled two 70-ton barges along the Forth and Clyde Canal in Scotland for 19.5 miles. The trip was successful, but the *Charlotte Dundas* was not used again. The canal company feared that the wash from the paddles would damage the banks.

So the story switches back to the United States, where the first commercial steamboat service was launched by Robert Fulton with the *Clermont* in 1807. In the following year the *Phoenix*, Fulton's second ship, became the world's first seagoing steamship. In 1812, Europe's first steamship passenger service was opened with the Scottish-built *Comet*.

Once steam had shown its possibilities, the eyes of the shipowners were on the Atlantic crossing. The American *Savannah* crossed in 1819, but she

Above: 17th-century admiral's galley. Very narrow and of shallow draught, these vessels carried two lateen sails and light artillery, but could only operate in fairly calm waters. Below: The English clipper *Cutty Sark*, 1869, 921 tons; and the American racing schooner *America*, which gave its name to the cup for ocean racing ships.

In the 1967 America Cup race, *Intrepid* won over *Columbia* by 7 minutes 45 seconds over a 24-mile course. In the above picture, they are passing each other; *Intrepid* having already rounded the buoy, is starting back upwind.

relied mainly on sails, using her paddles only occasionally. In 1827, the Dutch paddle steamer *Curacao* struggled across from Rotterdam to the West Indies in 22 days. Five years later the British *Rhadamanthus* crossed from Plymouth to Barbados, with stops at sea to de-salt the boilers. The first crossing under continuous steam power was made by the British packet ship *Sirius*, which in 1838 crossed from Ireland to New York in 18 days 10 hours.

Paddle steamers were not really satisfactory for ocean trips. They were not very fast, and their paddles were likely to be damaged by heavy seas. Several ships in the 1840's were fitted with a new invention, the propeller. The British Admiralty decided to fit propellers to all its steamships after a tug-of-war between propeller and pad-

dle-driven sloops in 1845. The propeller-driven sloop simply towed the paddle-driven one away stern first. The first propeller-driven Atlantic crossing was made in 1843 by the *Great Britain,* built by the engineer Isambard Brunel.

Steamships began to build up a reputation for reliability and speed. In most weather conditions, they could still keep to their timetables. The American Civil War saw the Confederates working hard to design faster ships to break the Northern blockade of their ports. Steamers with tapered hulls and reduced superstructures slipped out of Southern ports, their churning paddles driving them at speeds of 17 or 18 knots.

The choice between steam and sail for battleships was settled by the Civil War battle between the two steam-powered ironclads *Monitor* and *Merrimac* in 1862. Though far from being a glorious battle, it proved once and

for all that a sailing vessel would have stood no chance against either ship.

The need, then, in war and peace, was for speed and maneuverability on the water; and steam had provided this. Rapidly one improvement followed another—three-stage engines, which produced more power for the same amount of steam; steam turbines; twin propellers; oil-burning boilers. Each of

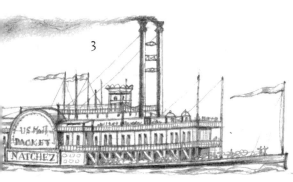

1. Boat designed by John Fitch in 1786; oars driven by steam.
2. The *Clermont*, 1807, built by Robert Fulton, was the first commercial paddle-wheel steamer, linking New York with Albany.
3. The *Mississippi*, 1870, one of the river steamboats that linked New Orleans with St. Louis; the *Mississippi* was still in service after World War I.
4. The *Great Western*, 1838.
5. The *Gloire*, France, 1859; this wooden vessel was covered with four-inch armor plating.

The *Great Eastern*, 27,000 tons, was 692 feet long, had a speed of 15 knots, and was the biggest transatlantic vessel of its time; it was used to lay the first transatlantic cable in 1865.

these, and further developments, gave a few more knots to every new ship. The turbine was the most important of these new inventions. In 1897, the English *Turbinia*, fitted with steam turbines and nine propellers, reached 34.5 knots. The race was on.

Battleships and Transatlantic Lines

At the beginning of this century, rivalry sprang up between the big shipping companies for the Blue Riband, the award for the fastest crossing of the Atlantic.

Around 1900, the German lines held the Riband with average speeds of 23 knots. In 1907 the English *Mauretania*

took it with 23.69 knots (27 mph). The *Mauretania* again broke the record in 1910 and held it until 1929. One attempt to gain the Blue Riband ended in one of the world's most terrible marine disasters. The White Star *Titanic*, then the world's largest liner, and considered to be unsinkable, sailed in April, 1912, on its maiden voyage from England to the United States. In the middle of the Atlantic it struck an iceberg at 22 knots and sank, with the loss of 1,500 passengers and crew.

The importance of speed in naval warfare was demonstrated at the battle of Tsushima, fought in May, 1905, between Japanese and Russian warships. The Japanese ships, mainly British-built, did five knots more than the

Russians. The extra five knots was more than enough to win the battle.

As a result of this, a new type of British battleship, the dreadnought, appeared in 1906. The first big warship to use turbines, the dreadnought attained a speed of 21 knots.

Naval battles of World War I, in particular the Battle of Jutland in 1916, were fought at speeds approaching 20 knots. The fastest of the large warships, the battle cruisers, reached almost 30 knots, an incredible speed considering that a battle cruiser is a vessel of 25,-000 tons. The speed of cruisers and destroyers increased in proportion, and this, coupled with their use of torpedoes, which themselves traveled at 25 to 30 knots, made them a deadly foe.

Speed, therefore, is of the greatest

Above: The first battle between armored ships took place in 1862 during the Civil War. At Hampton Roads, Virginia, the Southern *Merrimac*, despite its armor, was crippled by the fire of the little *Monitor* of the Union Navy.

Below: Dreadnought was the name of a new class of large and powerful battleships; this 1906 prototype was copied and improved upon by several navies before disappearing as a fighting ship after World War II.

importance. The fastest ships can choose the time and the place for the fight—and can get quickly out of reach of danger if their luck runs out.

Speed between 1918 and 1945

Ships' performances went on improving after 1918, given an added boost by the launching in 1928 of the *Selandia*, the word's first ocean-going diesel-

Left: The first "greyhound of the seas," the *Mauretania*, built in 1907 by the Cunard Line. The *Mauretania*, 38,-000 tons, 780 feet long, and with a speed of 27.4 knots, held all transatlantic speed records until 1929.

powered vessel. The race for the Blue Riband continued. The German liner *Bremen* regained it in 1929 with 28 knots. In 1933, the Italian *Rex* took it with 29 knots. In 1935 it went to the French *Normandie,* with 30.3 knots, and in 1936 to the English *Queen Mary,* with 30.6 knots. World War II interrupted the race, but vessels like the *Queen Mary* continued to cross the oceans as troop transports, needing every knot of Blue Riband speed to avoid the torpedoes of enemy submarines.

The treaty signed at the Washington Conference of 1922 by the United States, Great Britain, France, Japan, and Italy restricted the size, speed, and armament of warships. The British battleships *Nelson* and *Rodney* were built to these new regulations and had a speed of 23 knots. By the Treaty of Versailles, signed after World War I, Germany was allowed to keep six battleships, which were not to be replaced by warships of more than 10,000 tons. The German answer was the "pocket battleships." Three of these heavy cruisers were launched after 1932—the *Deutschland,* the *Admiral Scheer,* and the *Admiral Graf Spee.* Because of

their powerful diesel engines, these ships could be heavily armored and carry bigger guns than was normal for a vessel of their size. They could also travel at 26 knots. So Germany had a medium-size ship, fast enough to get away from a battleship and heavily armed enough to blow a cruiser out of the sea.

When Hitler came to power in Germany in 1933, he felt bound by no treaty, and built the battleships *Scharnhorst* and *Gneisenau,* which had a speed of 32 knots. Two larger battleships, the *Tirpitz* and the *Bismarck,* were laid down in time for launching at the outbreak of war in 1939. They had a speed of more than 30 knots.

All this caught Britain and France napping. The British had only three old battle cruisers fast enough to catch a pocket battleship. All France's battleships were much too slow. So both countries began to build faster ships. The British built the *King George V,* of 29 knots; the French, two Dunkerque ships of 31 knots. So began the race that did not end until 1945.

During World War II, the fastest ships were the torpedo boats (M.T.B.s). The British M.T.B. could travel at 40

The *Savannah,* 20,000 tons, the first nuclear-powered merchant ship. Built in the United States and launched in 1959, it can cruise for 300,000 miles at 20 knots without refueling.

The Russian flagship *Suvarov* at the battle of Tsushima, off South Korea in 1905. The Russian fleet of Admiral Rojestvensky was almost completely destroyed, and the outcome of the war was decided.

knots, while the big heavy German *Schnellboote* did 39 knots. Fastest of all were the Italian M.A.S. boats, which could reach 50 knots.

The fastest destroyer was the French *Le Terrible,* which in 1935 reached a speed of 45.02 knots and which stayed on the active list until 1957.

World War II saw the dethronement of the battleship and its replacement by the aircraft carrier. Speed and accuracy were the reasons. A battleship, moving at 30 knots to get its guns within range of the enemy, could not possibly make contact as quickly as a ship traveling at the same speed which could launch its planes at 200 knots whenever it chose. And bombing enemy ships from directly overhead gave better results than firing guns at them from a distance of several miles.

Methods of Propulsion

Traveling on, or through, water has its special problems, the biggest of which is the water resistance to the vessel's hull. As engines get more powerful, hull shapes of commercial ships must be modified along with them if speeds and carrying capacity are to be increased.

A modern cargo vessel or tanker can travel at 16 to 20 knots. The great cargo ships of the *American Challenger* type, belonging to the United States Lines, travel the old Blue Riband route at 25 knots. Speeds of passenger liners across the Atlantic, although it is no longer officially a race, have far outstripped the best prewar speeds. The fastest crossing was made in 1952 by the American liner *United States.* On her maiden voyage she averaged

35.59 knots (40.98 mph) over the 2,949 nautical miles from the Ambrose Light Vessel, New York, to the Bishop Rock Light in the Scilly Isles. She made the full trip from New York to Le Havre, France, in 4.5 days. With this feat the *United States* broke the 31-knot record of the *Queen Elizabeth*. The French successor to the *Normandie*, the liner *France*, has been limited to 31 knots for its commercial runs, although on trials it reached 34.21 knots.

The other giants of the merchant fleets, and the ships most characteristic of our age, are the oil tankers. Constantly getting bigger and faster, they have reached their present limit in the Japanese *Universe Kuwait*, a monster 1,135 feet long and with a displacement of 312,000 tons. The tanker has a capacity of 2,200,000 barrels of oil.

Warships of conventional form have

Above: The motor torpedo boat *Brave Borderer* of the British Navy, introduced in 1948; with 10,500 horsepower, she reached 50 knots during trials.
Below: The American aircraft carrier *Forrestal*, 85,000 tons, until 1960 was the largest in the world, with a length of 1,100 feet. Its bridge alone, 252 feet wide, is more than big enough to hold the three ships in which Columbus reached America. Nuclear-powered (280,000 horsepower), the *Forrestal* has a speed of 34 knots, carries 3,412 men and 100 aircraft. An explosion and fire aboard the vessel took the lives of 134 men in 1967.

also gained in speed. The world's largest aircraft carrier, the nuclear-powered *Enterprise* launched in 1960, is able not only to carry 100 supersonic aircraft, but herself to travel at more than 35 knots (40 mph). Her escorts have to travel at this speed and faster in order to keep up with her.

Frigates, antisubmarine escorts, travel at more than 36 knots, because their underwater opponents have reached speeds that make antisubmarine vessels of less than 30 knots out of date.

The fastest ships of conventional hull design are still certain types of motor torpedo boats, like the *Brave Borderer* and *Ferocity* of the British Navy. These boats, thanks to the power provided by turbines developed from those used in aircraft, can travel at well over 50 knots.

The gas turbine and the atomic reactor will play an increasingly greater part in propelling ships of the future. The gas turbine works by having its vanes pushed around by jets of exploding gas. The tanker *Auris* was the first merchant ship to be fitted with a gas turbine, all her four diesel engines being replaced with one turbine in 1955.

The first nuclear-powered merchant ship, the Russian icebreaker *Lenin,* was launched in 1957. The *Lenin* can reach up to 18 knots in clear water and break ice 8 feet thick at 2 knots. The American nuclear-powered cargo ship *Savannah*, which made her first Atlantic crossing in 1964, can move at 20.5 knots, and can carry enough fuel to last for more than three years.

Records on Water: Speedboats and Hydrofoils

Because of the resistance offered by the water to a ship's hull, it is not surprising that the greatest speeds are achieved by those boats whose shape lifts most of the hull *out* of the water once the vessel is in motion.

Many designs for speedboat hulls have been, and are being, produced. And they all have one object in common—to leave as little of the craft as possible in contact with the water. Common features of many designs are a sharply pointed bow to cleave a passage for the craft, and a redan, or step, about halfway along the bottom of the hull to help the boat to "plane" over the surface. At about 120 mph, a boat hardly touches the water at all. It is moving mainly on a cushion of air.

The great danger of high speed on water is that the boat may suddenly go out of control. At 200 mph, the effect of hitting even the smallest wave can be disastrous. The boat can be sent into an uncontrollable "looping," or shot straight into the air to come diving back bow first into the water, wrecking the boat and almost certainly killing the pilot.

The battle cruiser *Strasbourg*, 1936, and its sister ship the *Dunkerque* (26,500 tons) marked the resumption of armored shipbuilding by the French after World War I.

Donald Campbell was killed in January, 1967, when *Bluebird* somersaulted backward at a speed estimated to be more than 328 mph. Like John Cobb, who died in 1952 when *Crusader* overturned at 207 mph, Donald Campbell lost his life in the never ending quest for speed.

Because of the dangers of rough waters, attempts to better speed records are made on sheltered lakes, never in the open sea. Although Campbell achieved the highest speed on water on his last and fatal run, the official record is 285.21 mph. This is the average of two runs made over a one-mile course by Lee Taylor, an American, in the jet-engined hydroplane *Hustler* on Lake Guntersville, Alabama, in 1967.

The world record for a conventional propeller-driven craft is 200.42 mph, set by Roy Duby of the United States in a Rolls-Royce engined hydroplane on Lake Guntersville in April, 1962.

The fastest speed achieved by a diesel-powered boat is 60.21 mph by Sir Max Aitken, in *Delta* 37, fitted with Cummin's engines, off Southampton, England, in March, 1966.

A boat design that promises a great deal for the future (although the idea itself dates back to 1891) is the hydrofoil. At high speed, the hull is lifted clean out of the water by the "foils" carried on stiltlike legs. Although a hydrofoil looks delicate and not very stable, it really is quite the opposite. The foils, which carry propellers and rudders, work in the calm water under the waves and are unaffected by rough conditions on the surface.

Research is going on into the possibilities of building larger and larger hydrofoils. The world's largest at present is a Norwegian craft capable of carrying 150 passengers and 8 cars. The fastest, the *HTC*, developed by Boeing in the United States, can travel at more than 114 mph. The Russian hydrofoil *Sputnik*, 107 tons, can carry 300 passengers at more than 60 mph. In the hydrofoil design, shipbuilders have speed and size, and they are working at increasing both.

The Italian hydrofoil *Freccia D'Oro*; this type of craft is ideal for swift travel between lakeside and coastal towns.

Speed
under Water

Submarines, from the **Turtle**
to the **Skipjack**

Although we often look upon the
submarine as a fairly modern invention, it has a history going back almost
350 years. The very first was probably
the rowboat, covered with leather,
whose ability to submerge was demonstrated by the Dutch scientist Cor-
nelius van Drebbel in England about
1620.

In the 18th century, several inventors
produced designs and prototypes of
underwater craft which, unfortunately,
usually drowned or suffocated their
crews. The inventors regarded the submarine mainly as a naval weapon, to
be used for underwater attacks on
enemy fleets. But until the development of the torpedo in 1868 by the
British engineer Robert Whitehead,
these weird underwater vessels had
hardly more than nuisance value. They
could be propelled only by human muscle power, moving at a snail's pace and
exhausting the crew in the process,
and they were limited to attacking
ships at anchor. When they reached
an anchored ship, there was the further problem of blowing it up, either
by attaching the explosive to the hull
or hurling it on a long pole, and then
getting away to a safe distance before the explosion actually happened.

In 1775, David Bushnell built his
weird one-man craft, the *Turtle*. In the
following year, during the American

Revolution, an American soldier used
the *Turtle* in an unsuccessful attempt
to blow up the British warship *Eagle*
in New York Harbor. Robert Fulton,
the paddle-boat builder, was given
money in 1800 by Napoleon Bonaparte,

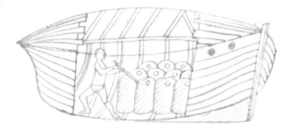

Above: Underwater cargo boat designed by the
physicist Marjotte in 1759. Below: the *Turtle*,
designed by the American colonist David Bushnell; this ingenious midget submarine made an
unsuccessful attempt to sink a British warship
during the American Revolution.

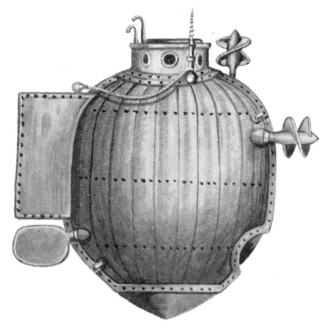

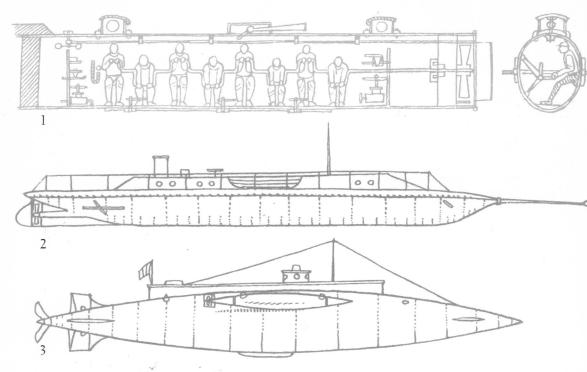

(1) The *Hunley*, 1864, was the first submarine to succeed in sinking a surface ship. (2) The *Plongeur*, 1863, a French submarine, carried ballast in the false bottom; it was armed with a mine carried on a pole; underwater, its balance was bad. (3) The *Gymnote*, 1889.

to build the submarine *Nautilus*. *Nautilus* was a success, but by the time it was built, Napoleon had decided he did not want it after all. In the War of 1812, another of Bushnell's submarines made another attack (again unsuccessful) on a British warship. A German soldier, Wilhelm Bauer, designed two submarines, one in 1851 that promptly sank, and another in 1855 that had better luck. The first successful submarine

attack on a warship was during the Civil War in 1864 when the Confederate submarine *Hunley* rammed a Union corvette. The *Hunley*, however, sank with its victim.

During World War I, both sides used submarines. The German U-Boats, with six torpedo tubes and a crew of

The giant submarine *Surcouf*, 1939, was revolutionary in design, with its folding airplane hangar and its double turret; it displaced 3,250 to 4,300 tons.

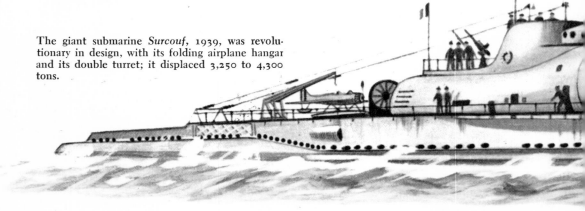

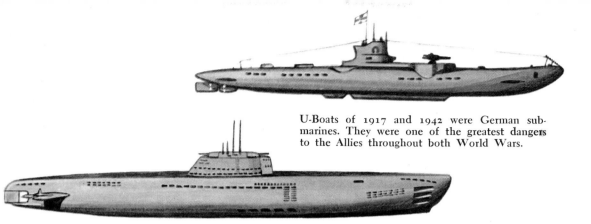

U-Boats of 1917 and 1942 were German submarines. They were one of the greatest dangers to the Allies throughout both World Wars.

45, could travel at 7 knots under water and 17 knots on the surface. The submarines of World War II were little different. By 1943, however, torpedoes could travel at 45 knots, could find their targets by sound, and could be detonated either magnetically or by impact.

In 1944, when the German submarine fleet found itself losing the battle against air and surface attacks that were aided by sonar and radar tracking devices, it looked for means of regaining the initiative. The result was several great improvements. First was the Schnorkel breathing tube, which allowed the submarine to use its diesel engines under water (previously it had used diesel engines on the surface and switched to electric engines under water). Improved design, coupled with increased power from electric motors, resulted in the XXI-type submarines which had an underwater speed of 16 to 17 knots, as against the normal 8 to 10. Then came the Walter motor,

worked by heat obtained by mixing concentrated hydrogen peroxide with water; this produced an underwater speed of 25 knots. The XXI-type submarines and the Walter motor came too late to be of any real use to the Germans in the war. They did, however, give a great boost to postwar submarine development.

Nuclear-powered Submarines

Less than ten years after the war came the greatest advance of all, the atomic submarine. The world's first was the American *Nautilus*, launched in 1954. With a radius of action of 40,000 nautical miles, a crew of 101, and a speed of 21 knots, her performance was so impressive that the United States government has since built several dozen nuclear-powered submarines of different types. Each carries 16 guided missiles and four torpedo tubes. In 1958, the *Nautilus* sailed under the ice of the North Pole. In

1960, the nuclear-powered *Triton* sailed around the world under water, cruising about 41,500 miles in 84 days. The *Triton*, 447 feet long, 37 feet wide, and with a crew of 148, can travel at 33 knots. The fastest submarines in the world are the nuclear-powered Skipjack-class vessels of the U.S. Navy, shaped like a stretched-out drop of water, which can travel under water at more than 45 knots. The drop-shaped hull is not very stable on the surface, but this matters little when the vessels spend so much of their time submerged.

Atomic submarines play a great part in present-day naval thinking. The United States, Britain, France, and the U.S.S.R. have them. Their importance lies not only in the fact that they can travel long distances under water but also in the fact that without even coming to the surface they can launch guided missiles like the *Polaris*, which have a range of 2,875 miles. The missiles are shot from the submarine by compressed air and ignite when they clear the water.

There are even antisubmarine submarines that can move at 35 knots to seek out their prey under water and are armed with torpedoes fitted with homing heads.

Below: The French bathyscaph *Trieste* of Auguste Piccard and his son, Jacques. Jacques, with Don Walsh of the United States, reached the bottom of the deepest known ocean trench, 35,800 feet.

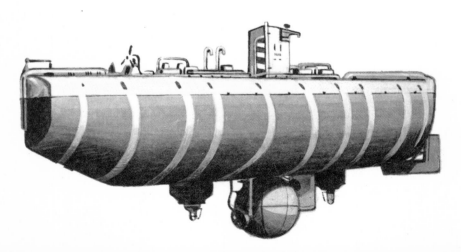

The *Nautilus*, the first American nuclear-powered submarine, was followed by several others. It became famous for the first journey under the ice of the North Pole in 1958.

Tomorrow:
The Commercial Submarine?

Submarines are still thought of mainly as weapons of war, the purpose for which the first clumsy and inefficient ones were designed. But a new concept is emerging, that of the submarine as a fast, safe, and economical carrier of goods and passengers.

Far under the surface, cruising through the still deeps, the submarine is not at the mercy of winds, waves and tides as the surface ship is. In time—although at present the apparatus is too costly—nuclear submarines will travel on regular commercial runs across the oceans, carrying cargoes more quickly, with less energy, and with greater regularity than surface vessels.

In the early 1960s, Jacques Cousteau began building underwater stations to which divers can return between dives. Since decompression is necessary only before returning to the surface, the divers are able to work for many hours per day instead of about one hour. Sometimes they stay under water for several weeks.

A tourist submarine is already operating in Lake Geneva, Switzerland. Future passengers across the Atlantic may well choose submarine travel for the simple reason that one does not get seasick under water.

The size of the commercial submarine is one of the problems to be resolved. To carry as much cargo as a surface ship, it would have to be immense. One answer seems to be for the submarine to tow its load in a string of underwater barges, some of which could be released outside the port they were bound for, while the submarine cruised on with the rest to the next destination. Underwater tankers carrying oil in this way would certainly be safer than surface tankers; it would be impossible for fire to break out, for instance, in containers a hundred fathoms down.

As well as carrying the products of the land, the submarine will be used to harvest the riches of the sea. Oil, minerals, and fish are there to be had in great quantities, and it will be the task of the submarine to help collect them. One day, fish will be farmed in much the same way as land animals— protected by man, fed by man, and finally rounded up by him for market. The submarine, and at greater depths the bathyscaph, will be used for this in much the same way as tractors and Jeeps are used in agriculture on dry land.

The bathyscaph, the invention of the Swiss scientist Auguste Piccard, can take man into the deepest parts of the sea. In 1960, a bathyscaph piloted by Piccard's son Jacques and a companion reached a depth of more than six miles. The Frenchman Jacques Cousteau has also used the bathyscaph for much underwater observation. In 1965, he conducted an experiment in which his crew lived for almost a month on the bottom of the Mediterranean in a specially designed underwater "house." They were able to leave the house, wearing diving equipment, to perform tasks such as dismantling the cap of an oil well at a depth of 375 feet.

The submarine has come an unbelievably long way since it was a leather-covered rowboat. But its story, far from being over, is just beginning.

CHAPTER SEVEN

Speed in the Air

Flight has been one of man's oldest and most persistent dreams. The more it eluded him, the more determined he became to achieve it.

The power of his brain and the skill in his hands gave him many advantages. His weapons turned him into a deadly hunter, his inventions gave him strength far beyond the power of his own muscles, his taming of the horse gave him the speed of the swiftest stallion. He could sail on the water and swim under it.

But, until quite recently, he could not fly.

In 1967, just over 60 years after the world's first clumsy powered flight, the American X-15A research plane reached a speed of 4,534 mph. This fantastic aircraft has been designed eventually to reach 5,455 mph, and it

George Cayley's helicopter, beginning of the 19th century.

flies so high (more than 50 miles) that it is almost a spaceship. Its pilot has actually been awarded astronaut's wings. The year 1961 saw the first successful manned space flight. Yuri Gagarin of the U.S.S.R. circled the earth in Vostok I at a maximum speed of 17,560 mph. In 1966, the American astronauts Charles Conrad and Richard Gordon, Jr., set up the record speed of 17,943 mph for a manned space flight.

We shall discuss space flight fully in the next chapter. Closer to earth was the feat in 1964 of 18 Lockheed F104 fighters, which left California, flew across the United States, crossed the Atlantic, and landed in Spain in less than 12 hours. They had flown more than 6,200 miles, nearly a quarter of the way around the world. This flight, which involved refueling nine times in mid-air, was made for military purposes, to test the possibilities of rapid intervention by air into a far dis-

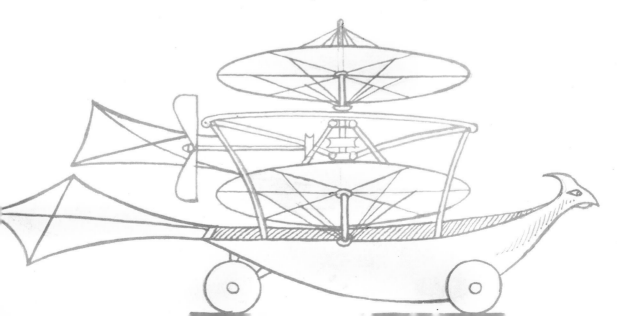

tant conflict. In the same year, the United States Air Force transported 16,000 men in two days from Texas to Germany in the operation "Big Lift." Both these achievements, like so many others made for military reasons, have provided information that will help to further the progress of civil aviation.

Every day there are more examples of service to humanity made possible by the speed of the airplane. People suddenly taken ill or hurt in an accident are rushed to the hospital by plane or helicopter; specialists are flown from distant places to the patient's bedside in a matter of hours; rare drugs are flown across the globe to be used in time to save a life; food and medical supplies are rushed to the victims of fire, flood, and earthquake in regions hardly accessible by land. Every minute saved in emergencies like these gives doctors and rescue workers valuable time in which to save lives.

Less dramatic, but almost as important, is the part the airplane and helicopter play in carrying materials for building dams, railway lines, and power stations to remote or mountainous parts of the earth. Whole regions can be transformed, and the lives of their inhabitants made much more safe and comfortable, in an incredibly short time.

From Mythology to Balloons

Man realized thousands of years ago that if he were to travel really fast, he would have to get off the ground.

The first manned free flight. In November, 1783, in a Montgolfier balloon, Pilâtre de Rozier and the Marquis d'Arlandes of France made a flight lasting 25 minutes. They covered 5.5 miles and reached a height of 3,300 feet.

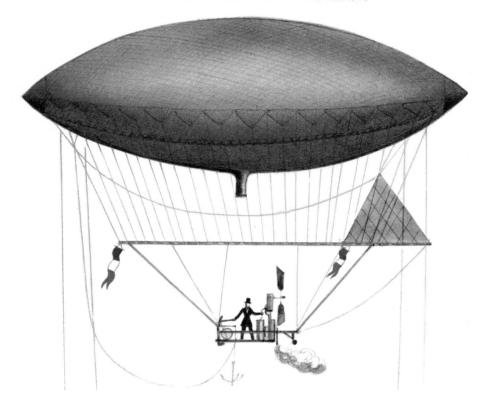

The first successful flight of a mechanically propelled balloon was made in September, 1852, by the French engineer Henri Giffard. The craft was 144 feet long and driven by a three-horsepower steam engine.

In many ancient legends, the heroes had magical powers of flight, and in some cases, like that of Mercury, messenger of the gods, actually used wings. The ancient Greek legend of Daedalus and his son, Icarus, tells how Daedalus made two pairs of wings to enable them to escape from imprisonment on the island of Crete. The story ended tragically because Icarus, overjoyed at finding himself able to fly, flew too near the sun. The heat melted the wax that held the feathers together, and he fell into the sea, leaving his father to fly on alone to Sicily.

Many later writers were fascinated by the possibilities of flight. Some wrote stories of pure fantasy, others made practical suggestions for getting airborne. In the middle of the 13th century, an English monk and scientist named Roger Bacon put forward ideas for building both a flapping-wing ma-

chine and a lighter-than-air machine. Some early writers looked even further ahead than this and predicted space travel. The English writer Francis Godwin wrote a novel called *The Man in the Moon* in 1638, and in 1648, the French writer Cyrano de Bergerac wrote *A Voyage to the Moon*. Leonardo da Vinci produced designs for flapping-wing aircraft that used both leg and arm muscles, fixed-wing aircraft, and even helicopters.

Progress toward flight was delayed for hundreds of years because most of the early birdmen tried to be exactly that. They insisted on copying the flapping flight of birds, not realizing that human arm muscles are not strong enough to support the weight of the body in flight. Even after 1680, when the Italian G. A. Borelli pointed this out, men still leaped from towers or high buildings with wings tied to their

81

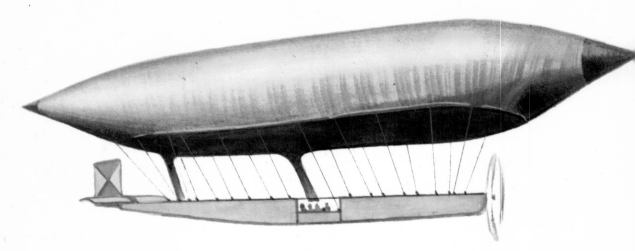

The first air circuit over a planned route in a dirigible. In August, 1884, the dirigible La France, piloted by its inventors, Captain Charles Renard and Arthur Krebs, flew five miles and came back to land at the point of departure. Driven by an 8 horsepower Krebs electric motor, La France was 165 feet long.

arms and flapped frantically all the way down to the inevitable crash landing.

All over the world, brave but foolhardy birdmen were falling to their deaths. Some, however, did make short flights, if we can believe the old chroniclers. An Englishman named Oliver of Malmesbury was said in 1020 to have flown one eighth of a mile.

In Turkey, at the beginning of the 17th century, Hezarfen Celebi was said to have flapped down from a tower into the marketplace of Scutari in Constantinople. There was an undignified end to the flight of the French Marquis de Bacqueville in 1742. Leaping from a tower in an attempt to fly across the River Seine, he crashed down onto a washerwoman's barge, breaking his leg.

While the birdmen were having such bad luck, others were working on the idea of lighter-than-air machines. Roger Bacon's idea for a machine that would float in air as lighter objects float on water, was taken up in the 1670s by a Jesuit priest named Fran-

cesco de Lana. Lana proposed pumping the air out of large copper globes to make them lighter than the air around them. The flaw in his theory was that the copper would have to be so thin that the outside air pressure would crush the globes as soon as the air inside was pumped out. Lana lost interest in trying to solve this problem, because he realized that a flying machine could be used in wartime to attack defenseless cities and innocent people.

The first real conquest of the air was left to two French papermakers, the brothers Joseph and Etienne Montgolfier. They were intrigued by the fact that a paper bag, dropped open end first over a fire, would rise, and they decided to experiment on a larger scale. (The reason the bag rose, of course, was that hot air, being lighter than cool air, rises, and it will carry a paper bag with it.)

In June, 1783, the Montgolfier brothers launched a 33-foot-diameter balloon made of paper and taffeta. It was filled with hot air by burning straw under its base. The balloon rose 6,000 feet and traveled for almost a mile and a half. In August, the Parisian physicist Jacques Charles successfully launched a silk balloon, 12 feet in diameter, filled with hydrogen. Because hydrogen is lighter than air, it had the same result as filling the balloon with hot air. In September, the Montgolfiers sent their first passengers—a duck, a rooster, and a sheep—on a flight. The balloon and its doubtless terrified crew landed safely after an eight-minute trip.

The first human being to leave the ground in a balloon was Jean Francois Pilâtre de Rozier, who went up in a captive (that is, tethered) Montgolfier balloon in October, 1783. November of that year saw the first manned free flight, when de Rozier and the Marquis d'Arlandes flew 5.5 miles across Paris in 25 minutes.

De Rozier and another passenger were to become the first victims of an air crash. In June, 1785, his balloon caught fire during an attempt to cross the English Channel. The tragedy pointed out the inescapable hazards of flying in a fragile alum-coated cotton envelope under which a red-hot brazier was burning, and led to the abandonment of the Montgolfier balloons in favor of gas bags filled with hydrogen. Hydrogen made ballooning much safer. But although the brazier was done

away with, there were still dangers. The gas itself was highly flammable and needed very little encouragement to burst into flames.

In January, 1785, J. P. Blanchard and John Jeffries had made the first crossing by air of the English Channel. Their trip, from Dover to Calais in a hydrogen balloon, showed that international flight was possible. But it also made balloonists keenly aware of their vessels' basic drawback. They could not be steered and were at the mercy of whichever wind happened to be blowing at the time.

By this time, the answers had already been thought of by the Frenchman Jean-Baptiste Meusnier. His idea was to stretch out the balloon into a fat cigar shape and fit it with a gadget he had invented called the propeller. The propeller was something that aviators would one day have cause to thank Meusnier for. At the time, however, it was not effective, because nobody had invented an engine powerful enough to turn it yet light enough to be lifted by

The German inventor Count Ferdinand von Zeppelin built a series of great dirigibles. The Graf Zeppelin made a world tour in 22 days before being put into regular service between Europe and South America in 1929. The burning of the Hindenburg (shown below) in 1937 ended the age of the airship.

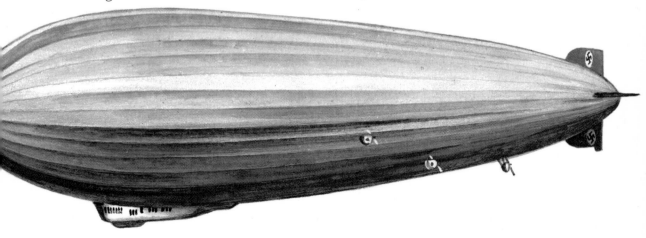

a balloon. For fifty years the progress of the balloon marked time, although it was used increasingly in warfare for observing enemy troop movements.

In October, 1797, the first parachute jump from a balloon was made when A. J. Garnerin leaped out 6,200 feet above the city of Paris.

In September, 1852, the first successful airship appeared in the sky. Built by the French engineer Henri Giffard, driven by a propeller powered by a 3-horsepower steam engine, it covered the 17 miles from Paris to Trappes at a steady 5 mph. Giffard's airship was cigar-shaped, and could be turned from a straight course by a rudder. The engine was not powerful enough, however, to turn the craft around against the wind.

The first air mail was carried in 1859 by balloonist John Wise of the United States. Along with several passengers, he traveled from Saint Louis to Henderson, New York, a distance of nearly 806 miles, at a speed of 37 mph. There was

In this glider, the German engineer Otto Lilienthal made more than 2,000 aerial descents between 1890 and 1896 over distances of up to 300 yards.

a strong wind throughout the journey and the navigators ran into a frightful storm over Niagara Falls.

In 1862, the Englishmen James Glaisher and Henry Coxwell reached a height of about 5.5 miles. They were lucky to come down alive, because until then nobody had realized the dangers of flying in the rarefied air high above the earth. French astronomer Camille Flammarion showed, before the outbreak of the Franco-Prussian War of 1870, how free balloons could be used to bring back information about the

In October, 1890, the French pioneer Clement Ader left the ground in a heavier-than-air mechanically propelled aircraft. This flight, however, was not sustained nor properly controlled, and thus does not qualify as the first airplane flight. The Eole had a four-bladed bamboo propeller driven by a steam engine, a wing span of 46 feet, and a length of 21 feet.

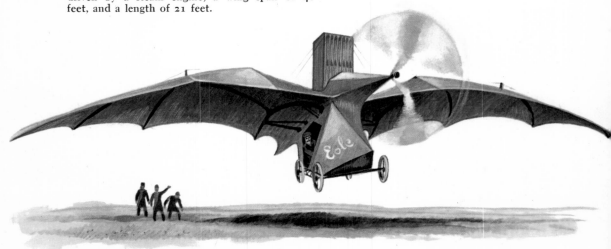

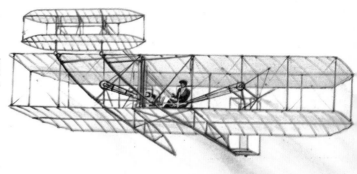

At Kitty Hawk, North Carolina, on December 17th, 1903, the Wright brothers made the first sustained flight in a heavier-than-air machine with mechanical propulsion.

The first town-to-town flight was made in January, 1908, by Henri Farman in a biplane built by the Voisin brothers in France.

atmosphere. After the war—during which balloons were used frequently as observation platforms—several attempts were made to build a dirigible, an airship that could be steered, but for a long time nobody had any success. Then, in August, 1884, Captains Charles Renard and A. C. Krebs made a 5-mile flight near Paris in their airship La France. Powered by an electric motor, the 165-foot-long, streamlined craft reached a speed of 14 mph and could be steered successfully. The dirigible had arrived.

After La France came many more airships, each an improvement on the one before. In France a series of magnificent machines was built by Henri Julliot and Alberto Santos-Dumont. In 1897, an Austrian engineer, David Schwartz, then living in Berlin, built the first rigid airship, one whose gas bag was supported from the inside by a metal framework. Though Schwartz's machine crashed on its third flight, it was to have a great influence on the work of the man whose name is automatically linked with that of the airship—the German Count Ferdinand von Zeppelin. Although Zeppelin's first two airships could hardly be called successful (one of them was wrecked by a storm after its first flight), he persevered, and by 1914 had built 26 airships, some of which could fly at 50 mph. Zeppelin's machines carried many thousands of passengers in Germany before World War I. When war broke out they were put to less peaceful use, bombing French and English cities.

Meanwhile, airship construction had been going on in both England and the United States. As well as large craft, the British had built small ones called "blimps" for use at sea to protect convoys and seek out submarines.

After the war, the success of Zeppelin's ships led Britain and the United

In July, 1909, Louis Blériot of France crossed the English Channel in a monoplane driven by a small 23-horsepower engine. He covered the 23 miles from the Pas-de-Calais to Dover in 37 minutes at a height of 400 feet.

States to copy them. The first trans-atlantic airship flight was made by one such craft, the British R-34, which in 1919 made the round trip of more than 6,000 nautical miles in 75 hours.

Airships grew bigger and bigger during the 1920s and early 1930s. The U.S. Navy's Los Angeles, built for them by the Germans in 1924, was 658 feet long. The Shenandoah, built in 1923, was 680 feet long and 79 feet across. The German Graf Zeppelin, built in 1928, was 775 feet long, 100 feet across, and could carry 50 passengers at more than 70 mph. And in 1936 came one of the biggest ever built, the German Hindenburg. The first airship to be fitted with diesel engines, the Hindenburg was 812 feet long, 135 feet across, and could travel at 78 mph.

The 1930s began with what promised to be the Golden Age of the airship. Within seven years, however, a series of terrible disasters caused its abandonment as a passenger-carrying vehicle. Though extremely comfortable and pleasant to travel in, the airship was still basically a cabin slung under a gigantic envelope of gas. The size of this envelope made the craft extremely vulnerable in storms, and its content, though the use of helium instead of hydrogen had cut down the fire risk, made it a death-trap if fire broke out.

The British R-101, 777 feet long, crashed in France during a storm, killing 46 out of the 54 passengers and crew. Britain lost interest in airships and the R-101's sister ship, R-100, was dismantled. Two sister airships of the U.S. Navy—the Akron and the Macon, crashed with tragic results. The Akron was destroyed by a storm in 1933, killing 73 people. The Macon crashed in the Pacific in 1935, killing two. After that, the United States stopped building rigid airships. In 1937, disaster overtook the mighty Hindenburg. As it landed in the United States during a storm, it burst into flames and exploded. There were no more regular airship flights from Germany.

Many blimps were used in World War II, and proved highly effective in submarine detection. But the basic faults of the large airships still remain. And it seems now that their day is over.

The First Heavier-than-Air Machines

While the early balloonists were floating triumphantly high above the ground, other inventors concentrated

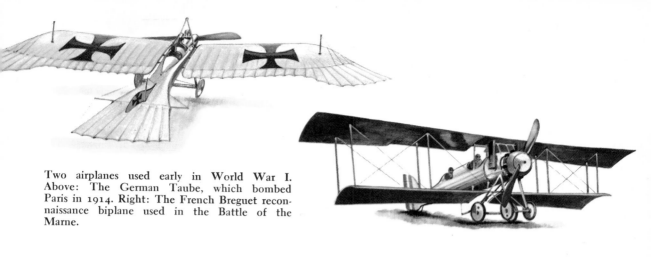

Two airplanes used early in World War I. Above: The German Taube, which bombed Paris in 1914. Right: The French Breguet reconnaissance biplane used in the Battle of the Marne.

on the apparently impossible—the building of a heavier-than-air machine that would fly.

Models of a helicopter had been made in France as early as 1460. Thirty years later Leonardo da Vinci drew up designs for an aerial propeller. But the first heavier-than-air machine known to leave the ground was the model helicopter built by the Frenchmen Launoy and Bienvenu in 1784.

For the next twenty years nothing happened, though inventors all over Europe were producing one impractical design after another. Then, in 1804, the Englishman Sir George Cayley built and flew successfully a model glider. Only five feet long, the glider was based on the principle of the kite, and was certainly nothing exciting to look at. But it laid down the basic shape for the airplane of today; it had an inclined kite for wings and a tail unit that included an elevator and a rudder.

By 1809, Cayley had built a full-size glider that flew unmanned. This could have been the real starting point for heavier-than-air flight, but the glider was wrecked and Cayley lost interest, spending the next thirty-odd years working on other projects. He came back to gliding in the 1850s, and built

a machine that carried his coachman across a valley. Although he was the first airplane pilot in history, the terrified coachman did not think much of the distinction. He stepped from the glider and immediately resigned.

Cayley's work meanwhile had inspired another Englishman, W. S. Henson. With another engineer, John Stringfellow, Henson built a 20-foot-long model of an "aerial steam carriage." This machine, weird though it looked, had many of the features of later aircraft—twin propellers, fuselage, undercarriage, rudder, elevator, and braced wings. Henson's model, however, never left the ground, and public ridicule made him give up the whole idea.

The first successful powered airplane was a model built by a French naval officer, Felix du Temple; it flew in 1858. In 1874, du Temple went on to build a full-size powered plane in which a sailor left the ground for a short time after the airplane had gained speed by being run down a ramp.

Other European inventors made hops of up to 200 feet, skimming just a few feet above the ground. The French inventor, Clement Ader, flew 164 feet in 1890, and in 1897 he covered 328 yards.

Between 1890 and 1896, Otto Lilienthal of Germany made more than 2,000 downhill glides, swinging his legs from side to side to control his machine. Lilienthal's effort produced many improvements in glider design, but his work ended tragically in a fatal crash in 1896. Others took up where Lilienthal left off, notably Octave Chanute of the United States, whose designs were much simpler and stronger. In 1893, the Australian Lawrence Hargrave invented the box kite, a toy that greatly influenced airplane design.

In the United States, in May, 1896, Samuel Pierpont Langley flew a steam-powered, pilotless model that reached more than 37 mph. A full-size version of the model did not leave the ground when it was tried out in 1903, but disappointment at this was quickly banished by happenings later in that year.

On the sand dunes of Kitty Hawk, North Carolina, on December 17th, 1903, the brothers Orville and Wilbur Wright made the world's first powered, sustained, and controlled flights. In their No. 1 Flyer they made four flights. In the best of these, Wilbur covered 852 feet into a strong wind in 59 sec-

onds. The actual distance through the air was half a mile, giving the plane a speed of just over 30 mph. The brothers were not content to rest on their laurels. They built other planes with even better controls. And on October 4th, 1905, their No. 3 Flyer stayed airborne for half an hour, banking, turning, and circling.

Progress in Europe, meanwhile, was still slow. Alberto Santos-Dumont flew 722 feet in 21 seconds in 1906. But it was not until October, 1907, that an aircraft flew for a full minute in Europe. This was achieved in France by Henri Farman who, in a Voisin biplane, at the same time set up a world speed record of 32.74 mph and a distance record of 3,368 feet. In 1908, Farman became the first man to fly an airplane from town to town and in 1909 the first to fly 100 miles. The first official flight in Britain did not take place until October, 1908, and then it was made by an American, Samuel Cody, who covered 1,390 feet.

France began to move ahead in aircraft design and several successful machines were built and flown. This work resulted in the flight that finally made

Aerial combat in 1916. A Nieuport II ("baby Nieuport") attacks a pair of German Albatrosses.

Above: Cauldron G4 twin-seater bomber, the first twin-engine plane in service in 1914. It flew from Paris to Rangoon, 6,800 miles, at an average speed of 52 mph in November, 1919.

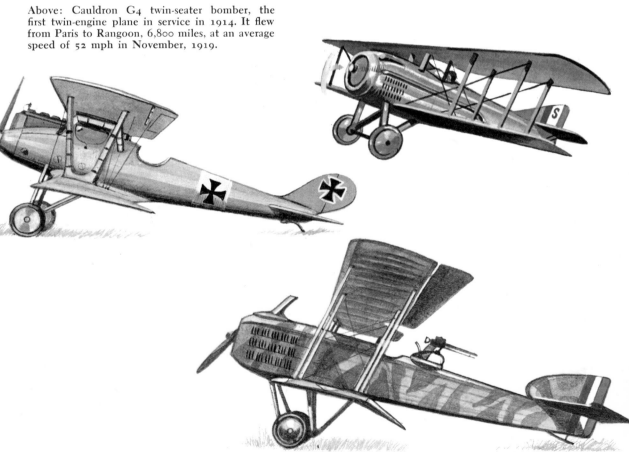

(1) Spad 7, fighter biplane, made its first appearance at the Battle of Verdun; its speed was 120 mph. (2) German single-seater fighter Pfalz D-XII, used in 1918, had a 160 horsepower motor and a speed of 115 mph. (3) Breguet 14A-2 twin-seater, used in 1917-1918 for reconnaissance and bombing; its speed was 112 mph.

On May 20th and 21st, 1927, Charles A. Lindbergh flew the Atlantic from west to east in the Spirit of St. Louis, covering 3,606 miles in 33 hours 30 minutes.

the world air-minded—the English Channel crossing by Louis Blériot. On July 25th, 1909, he flew his 23-horsepower monoplane, Blériot XI, from the Pas-de-Calais, France, to Dover in 37 minutes.

The following year was full of French successes in the air. Henri Fabre flew the first flying boat at 31 mph. In April, Louis Paulhan, in the biplane Henri-Farman, flew the 182 miles from London to Manchester, England, in 4 hours 12 minutes. In June, a flier named Martinet covered 26 miles in 31 minutes 55 seconds.

In September, 1913, Roland Garros crossed the Mediterranean from Saint-Raphaël to Bizerta on the coast of Africa in the 60-horsepower Morane Saulnier at an average speed of 62 mph. Two weeks later, Maurice Prévost set up a record of 126.75 mph in the 160-horsepower monoplane Deperdussin, a trim-looking craft whose design greatly influenced future construction.

The airplane had established itself, had proved its worth in performance and speed. Soon it was to show its mettle under harsher circumstances.

The First World War: From 37 to 150 mph

World War I saw airplane design, speed, and flying techniques leap ahead. Britain entered the war on August 4th, 1914. By October of that year, British aircraft were bombing German Zeppelin sheds. In the early bombing attacks, the pilots leaned over the edges of the cockpits and dropped the bombs by hand. Early fighter planes pursued each other with pilots taking potshots with rifles and revolvers. Soon, however, aircraft were being built for special roles—as bombers, fighters, and reconnaissance planes.

At the beginning of the war the speed of military planes was only about 37 mph. They were heavy with the weight

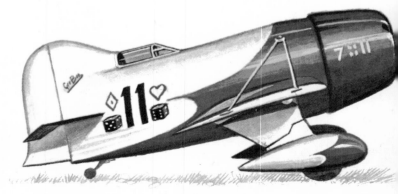

The Gee Bee. In this aircraft, in 1931, James Doolittle broke the world speed record with 293.5 mph.

Italian hydroplane Macchi-Castoldi 72 topped world speed records for all planes in April, 1933, with a speed of 423 mph.

of bombs, machine guns, armor plating, and sometimes extra crew members. Four years later, with stronger engines and improved design, they reached 150 mph.

The increase in the rate of aircraft construction, as well as the appalling losses, is illustrated by the fact that France built 41,500 aircraft and 64,000 engines during the war. After providing the Allies with 9,500 planes and 28,800 engines, she was left at the end of the war with only 3,600 aircraft. Germany ended the war with 15,000 planes. The British Royal Air Force ended the war with 22,647 aircraft and 291,170 officers and men. In 1914, the British had had 160 planes.

Fighter planes were developed on both sides to shoot down enemy bombers and reconnaissance planes and to defend those of their own side. The spotter planes were probably even more of a menace than the bombers, because the information they gained high above the battlefields made it possible for artillery barrages to be brought down with murderous accuracy. Fast, slim, and powerful fighter planes were built

to combat bombers. At first they operated singly, and by modern standards were not very effective. But, in 1915, a way was found of firing a machine gun through the propeller, and this led to dog fights between whole squadrons.

Leading fighter aces of the war were men like the German Count von Richthofen, with 80 "kills"; the French Colonel René Fonck, with 75; the British Captain Edward Mannock, with 73; and the American Captain Edward Rickenbacker, with 22.

The advent of the fighter forced the bombers to operate at night. Aircraft like the Voisin, Letord, and Farman, with a maximum speed of 72 mph, were too clumsy and slow to escape pursuit by day. Day bombing became possible, however, in the winter of 1917, with

Croix de Sud, French hydroplane, was used over the South Atlantic route from Paris to Brazil. It was lost in 1936.

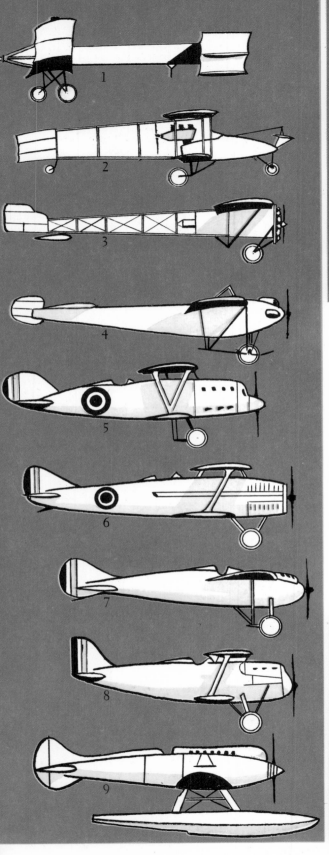

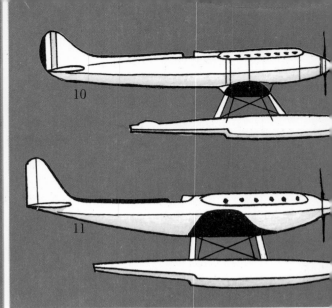

Air speed records up to 1957:

1. Santos-Dumont 14, piloted by Santos-Dumont, November 12th, 1906, 25.5 mph.
2. Farman-Voisin, piloted by Henri Farman, October 26th, 1907, 32.74 mph.
3. Blériot XII, piloted by Louis Blériot, August 28th, 1909, 46.5 mph.
4. Nieuport, piloted by Nieuport, June 21st, 1911, 82.5 mph.
5. Nieuport 29, piloted by Sadi-Lecointe, February 7th, 1920, 170.5 mph.
6. Spad 20, piloted by Casale, February 28th 1920, 175.5 mph.
7. Nieuport biplane, piloted by Sadi-Lecointe September 21st, 1922, 211.5 mph.
8. Curtiss R-6, piloted by B. C. Mitchell, October 13th, 1922, 222 mph.
9. Macchi M52, piloted by De Bamardi, November 30th, 1928, 317.5 mph

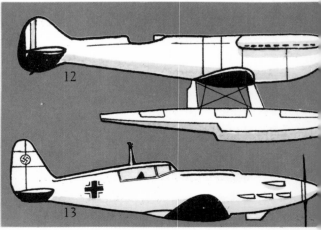

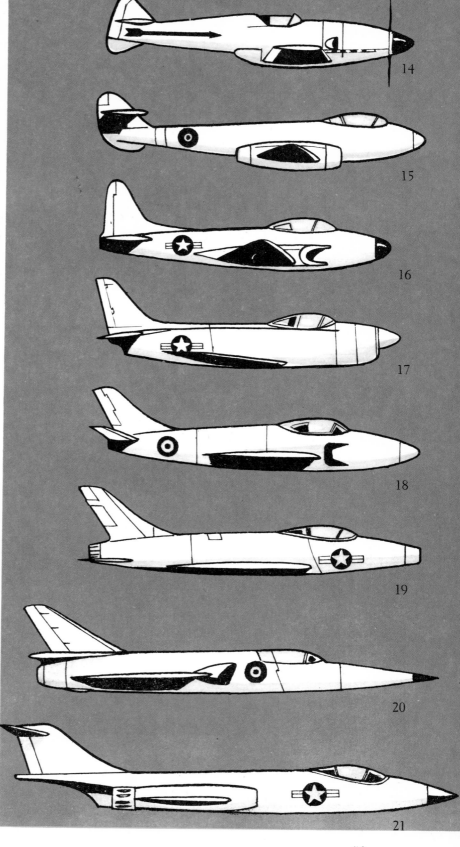

10. Gloster VI, piloted by Stainforth, September 10th, 1929, 335.5 mph.
11. Supermarine S6, piloted by Orlebar, September 12th, 1929, 356.5 mph.
12. Macchi 72, piloted by Agello, October 23rd, 1934, 440 mph.
13. Heinkel He 112, piloted by Dieterle, March 30th, 1939, 463 mph.
14. Messerschmitt Me 109, piloted by Fritz Wendel, April 27th, 1939, 469 mph.
15. Gloster Meteor IV, piloted by J. Wilson, September 7th, 1946, 601 mph.
16. Lockheed F8OR, piloted by A. Boyd, June 19th, 1947, 622.5 mph.
17. United States F86-D Sabre, piloted by J. S. Nash, November 19th, 1952, 698 mph.
18. Supermarine Swift FA4, piloted by Lithgow, September 25th, 1953, 752 mph.
19. United States F100C Super-Sabre, piloted by Hanes, August 20th, 1955, 822.1 mph.
20. Fairey Delta 2, piloted by P. Twiss, March 10th, 1956, 1,071.5 mph.
21. McDonnell F101 Voodoo, piloted by Drew, December 10th, 1957, 1,207 mph.

the introduction of the two-seater Bre-guet 14 B-2, whose 300-horsepower Renault motor gave it a speed of 130 mph, enough to escape from a fighter, given any kind of a start.

Another interesting development of the air war was the emergence of the seaplane, which was used to track down and bomb both submarines and surface ships. Flying boats carrying over 660 pounds of bombs could reach a speed of 86 mph. Fast Hanriot-Dupont seaplanes that could travel at 124 mph were used as lookouts for ships, scanning the skies for the first signs of approaching enemy bombers or fight-ers. The seaplane was to play a big part in the quest for speed in the air, once the war was over.

The Age of the Seaplane

The end of the war found Europe and America with more, bigger, and better aircraft, with factories tooled to produce them in large numbers, and with a great many trained pilots. Every-thing seemed to point toward an ex-pansion of civil flying—everything, that is, except customers. People had yet to be convinced that the advantages of flight outweighed the disadvantages and risks—the discomfort, the danger of crashing, the possibility of getting lost, the scarcity of airfields, and the irregu-larity of flights.

The answer to the lack of enthusiasm on the public's part seemed to be to promote speed contests, to demonstrate that flying was not only an increasingly fast method of travel, but an increas-ingly safe one.

In 1920, a converted and stripped-down Nieuport 29 fighter reached 187 mph. Three years later, the American flier, Brow, reached 258 mph in a Cur-

1

2

3

4

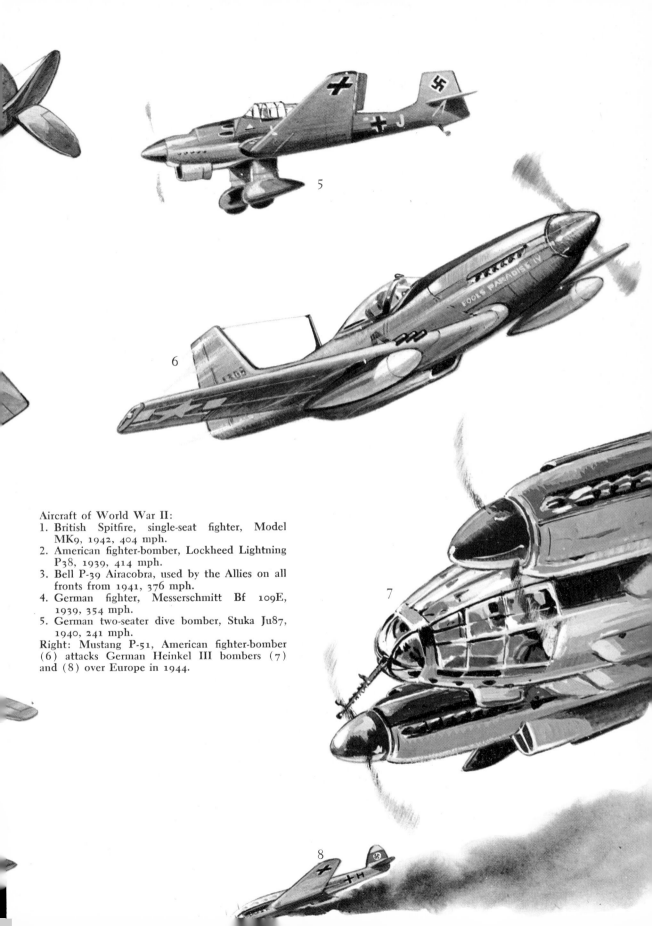

Aircraft of World War II:

1. British Spitfire, single-seat fighter, Model MK9, 1942, 404 mph.
2. American fighter-bomber, Lockheed Lightning P38, 1939, 414 mph.
3. Bell P-39 Airacobra, used by the Allies on all fronts from 1941, 376 mph.
4. German fighter, Messerschmitt Bf 109E, 1939, 354 mph.
5. German two-seater dive bomber, Stuka Ju87, 1940, 241 mph.

Right: Mustang P-51, American fighter-bomber (6) attacks German Heinkel III bombers (7) and (8) over Europe in 1944.

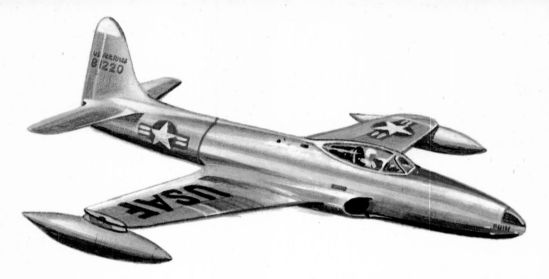

tiss. In 1924, the Frenchman Bonnet, in a Bernard-Ferbois, reached 278 mph. This record stood until 1931 when James Doolittle (eventually to become the famous General Jimmy Doolittle) flew at 293.5 mph in his Gee-Bee.

Doolittle's speed in a land plane, however, had already been bettered by seaplanes competing for the Schneider Trophy. This international seaplane race, first held in 1913, had a rule that gave the trophy forever to the country which won the race three successive times. Britain succeeded with wins in 1927, when S. N. Webster flew 282 mph; in 1929, when H. R. D. Waghorn flew 324 mph; and in 1931, when J. N. Boothman flew 340 mph. The planes that won the last two races were Super-

Lockheed Shooting Star F80, the first U.S. jet fighter, 1944; speed, 536.5 mph; ceiling, 44,400 feet.

marines S6, designed by Reginald Mitchell; they were the forerunners of the famous Spitfire fighter of World War II. After the trophy races in 1929 and 1931, the S6Bs broke the world records over a three-kilometer (1.86-mile) course. In 1929, Squadron Leader Orlebar reached 356.5 mph, and in 1931, Flight Lieutenant Stainforth averaged 407 mph; he was the first man to fly at more than 400 mph. By 1934,

Komet, the first rocket airplane, made by Messerschmitt, in flight in 1941; top speed, 596 mph; climbing speed, 30,020 feet in 2 minutes 30 seconds.

the seaplane had become even faster; its last propeller-driven record was the 440 mph reached in that year by the Italian, Agello, in a Macchi 72.

The seaplane was able to beat the wheeled airplane because it was designed primarily for flying. Landing presented no problems; it simply touched down on the nearest clear stretch of calm water. Wheeled planes, on the other hand, had at the time only short grass runways. Getting off the ground and safely back onto it meant that the design could not be concentrated solely on speed in the air. However, three ideas allowed wheeled planes to wrest the speed records back from seaplanes:

1. The high-lift flaps which, by altering the shape of the wing, could make it thin and flat for high speed, or into a high-lift airfoil for low speed.

2. The variable-pitch propeller, which allowed a rapid take-off in first gear, then high-speed flight in overdrive before landing slowly in first gear again. Today the variable-pitch propeller even allows reversing on the ground.

3. The retractable undercarriage, which allowed the wheels to be tucked away when in flight, so improving the streamlining of the plane.

With these improvements the wheeled aircraft regained its lead. In 1939, on the eve of World War II, Dieterle of Germany reached 463 mph in a Heinkel He 112, only to be overtaken by his fellow pilot Fritz Wendel with a speed of 469 mph in a Messerschmitt Me 109.

The First Jet Planes

The idea of jet propulsion was more than 2,000 years old by the time World War II began. A hundred years before Christ, a scientist called Hero, who lived in Alexandria, Egypt, built a simple engine called the *aeolipile* that worked by jets of steam.

Britain pioneered in applying jet propulsion to aircraft. In 1926, A. A. Griffith put forward his theories for using gas turbines to power aircraft. In 1928, a Royal Air Force cadet named Frank Whittle wrote a paper on the possibilities of jet propulsion, and in 1930, he patented a design for a jet engine.

Several countries began to investigate the possibilities of jet-powered flight in the 1930s. By 1937, Whittle's engines were being tested. In 1938, the French engineer, René Leduc, exhibited a model plane powered by a ramjet. In August, 1939, five days before the outbreak of war, the first jet plane to fly, the German Heinkel He 178, took to the air. It was followed in 1940 by the Italian Caproni-Campini CC2.

Above: Autogyro, Kellet KD-1 A, 1943, 126.5 mph. Below: Super-Frelon SA 3210, of the Sud-Aviation Company; the prototype was tested in December, 1962; speed, 161.5 mph; ceiling, 15,750 feet.

American helicopter Sikorsky S-61 N came into service in 1961; speed, 124 mph; ceiling, 7,890 feet.

These first two planes were not completely satisfactory, however, and the combatants still relied on piston-driven aircraft for the war in the air. Both fighters and bombers were fitted with tremendously powerful engines, and certain light bombers, such as the British Mosquito, which often exceeded 370 mph, were faster than the fighters that tried to intercept them. But there was a limit to the speed that could be reached by piston engines.

The first plane to fly successfully using a turbo-jet engine was the British Gloster E28/39, powered by a Whittle engine. In May, 1941, it had a top speed of 300 mph, which was later built up to 466 mph. In the following year, the Germans successfully flew a Messerschmitt Me 262, powered by a Junkers Jumo 004 jet engine. This plane, with a speed of 546 mph, went into action as the first jet-propelled combat aircraft. The Germans used a pulse-jet engine to power the pilotless V-1, or flying bomb, that was used in raids on London in 1944. The R.A.F. used piston-engined Tempests to shoot down the flying bombs, but soon had something better—the Gloster Meteor, Britain's first gas-turbine engined fighter.

By the end of 1944, both Britain and Germany were using jet fighters for air combat. By this time, too, Germany had produced the world's first jet bomber, the Arado.

The jet age, then, had its bloody beginning in the latter years of World War II. But speeds were still not great. At 590 mph, twice the speed of piston-engined fighters at the beginning of the war, jets were still nowhere near as fast as they were to be in a very few years' time.

The Birth of the Helicopter

World War II also saw the development of the helicopter from something regarded as a slightly crazy toy to a machine of great adaptability and usefulness.

We have already seen how ancient is the early history of the helicopter—da Vinci's design of 450 years ago, the French models of 1460, and those of Launoy and Bienvenu in 1784—but the machine took a long time to develop from these crude beginnings.

Several inventors during the 1800s built models that got off the ground, but the first full-size man-carrying machine was that launched by Louis and Jacques Breguet, of France, in September, 1907. Steadied by poles stuck in the ground, and held by four men as an extra precaution, the machine rose just a few inches. In November, 1907, the first man-carrying free flight was made, in a twin-rotor machine built by another Frenchman, Paul Cornu. Cornu's machine cleared the ground by a whole foot!

During and after World War I, designers worked to solve the problems posed by the helicopter, but so many were the failures that a controllable machine seemed an impossibility. However, in 1924, Pescara stayed in the air for 10 minutes and Œhmichen flew for more than half a mile. In 1923, Juan de la Cierva of Spain flew his autogiro (a machine with a conventional propeller and a rotor that operates by passage of air). It was far from successful, but it greatly contributed to helicopter design.

It was 1937 before the first fully controllable helicopter, the German Focke-Achgelis, appeared. This twin-rotor machine reached a speed of 76 mph, as against the 28 mph reached by that of Maurice Claysse a year earlier.

The first successful single-rotor helicopter was built in the United States by Igor Sikorsky in 1939. Sikorsky's machine proved so versatile that the American government ordered many for its armed forces. Progress has been kept up since the war, with many countries using helicopters for a multitude of jobs.

Because it is so versatile—able to fly up, down, backward, forward, or just hover on the spot—it would be unfair to expect the helicopter to fly as fast as conventional aircraft. The fastest speed reached was that of 217.8 mph, achieved in 1963 by the Frenchmen Jean Boulet and Roland Coffignot. Jean Boulet is also the holder of the helicopter altitude record with a height of 36,027 feet.

Sound and Heat Barriers

During the ten years after World War II, the turbo-jet made more progress than the piston engine had in fifty years. Jet propulsion proved its worth, with military aircraft as the testing ground, and has since replaced piston engines on most big civil aircraft as well as many of the smaller ones. Thrust has replaced horsepower. And one kind of jet after another has been tried and adopted—centrifugal jet, axial jet, double-flow jet, ramjet, turbo-jet, turbo-ramjet, and finally rocket propulsion.

As speeds increased, aircraft met the first great obstacle, the sound barrier. Flight near to the speed of sound, which is 760 mph at sea level, 660 mph

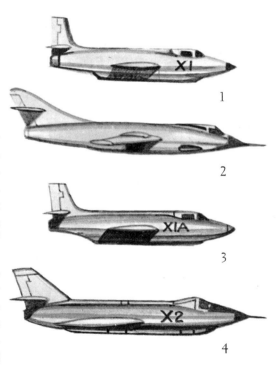

Records of American experimental aircraft:
1. Bell X-1, Mach 1.06 (714.5 mph), 1947.
2. Douglas Skyrocket, Mach 2.01 (1,316 mph), 1953.
3. X-1A, Mach 2.5 (1,639.5 mph), 1953.
4. Bell X-2, Mach 2.9 (1,888 mph), 1956.

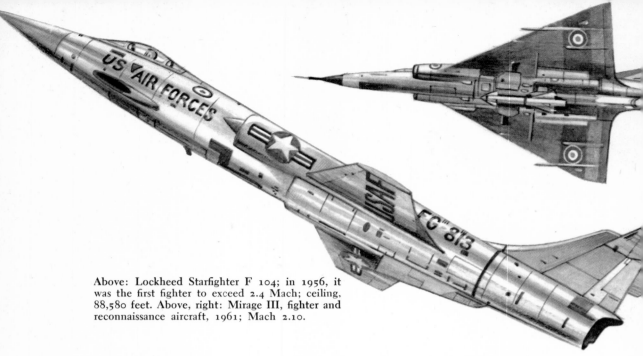

Above: Lockheed Starfighter F 104; in 1956, it was the first fighter to exceed 2.4 Mach; ceiling, 88,580 feet. Above, right: Mirage III, fighter and reconnaissance aircraft, 1961; Mach 2.10.

at 36,000 feet, causes air to build up in front of the plane and form a shock wave. If an aircraft wants to break this wave, it must fly at a speed much higher than the speed of sound.

The first plane to fly deliberately faster than sound in level flight was the United States Bell X-1, piloted by Captain Charles E. Yeager, in October, 1947. This did not qualify for an official record, however, because it was air-launched from a "mother" aircraft. The X-1 did not use jets, but a liquid fuel rocket motor.

In 1950, an American Sabre fighter broke the barrier, causing the famous supersonic bang. Because the instrument boards of the time did not include a machmeter (an instrument that tells the pilot how fast he is flying in relation to the sound speed of his particular location and altitude), the pilot did not know of his feat until he was told after he landed. For a long time the sound barrier held speed records back. Then, on August 20th, 1955, a Super-Sabre established the first official supersonic record, reaching 822.1 mph over a stretch of nine miles at a height of

more than 29,370 feet. The regulations had required that the test run should be over two miles and less than 250 feet from the ground, but this had to be changed because a flight made at such high speed and low level is too dangerous. Moreover, the jet could reach its full power only high above sea level, where air resistance is much less.

In 1956, the British Fairey Delta 2 was the first plane ever to fly at more than 1,000 mph, and by 1960, speeds of more than 1,500 mph were classified as almost commonplace.

With the increased speeds came changes in the shape of aircraft. Their wings became arrowlike at first, then took a delta shape, and became straight again only when designers managed to produce a profile thin enough, yet strong enough, for the straight shape at high speed. Today, thanks to improvements in design and the use of new metals, it is possible to make wings any shape for flight at twice the speed of sound.

Further up the speed scale, another barrier appeared—the heat barrier. Friction of the air against the skin of the plane causes the temperature to rise so much that conventional metals weaken and even melt. The front of the fuselage and the leading edges of the wings of a Mirage III, for example, reach a temperature of 150 degrees Fahrenheit when flying at Mach 2 (twice the speed of sound) at a height of over 39,000 feet. The famous American research aircraft, X-15, reaches 600 degrees on the fuselage and a minimum of 400 degrees on less exposed areas. The pilot's cabin must be refrigerated and fuel and equipment specially protected.

The heat problem becomes more and more serious as higher speeds are reached. The only answer is to develop metals that will resist these high temperatures, or to fly so high that the rarefied atmosphere creates very little friction. In theory, the ideal solution would be for planes to fly in an almost total vacuum, but this would be out of the question. Aircraft must travel through the denser layers of our atmosphere, if only to take off and land.

Supersonic Airplanes

Official world air speed records are not much guide to the real achievements of the fastest planes. Records are broken nowadays mainly by military aircraft and the countries concerned are, naturally, reluctant to reveal precise speeds of machines still on the secret list. The official world air speed record, 2,070.1 mph set up by Colonel Robert Stephens and Lieutenant Colonel Daniel Andre, U.S.A.F., in a Lockheed YF-12A, on May 1, 1965, is being beaten almost daily by research aircraft. For example, the American X-15 has consistently flown at speeds over 4,000 mph and is designed to reach speeds of more than 5,000 mph.

It is far easier to keep up with the progress of civil aircraft. Companies which own or produce a fast plane are only too eager to let everyone know about it. In commercial civil aviation, as in military, the piston engine has virtually disappeared. The highest speed claimed for a piston-engined aircraft was the 504 mph reached in 1944 by

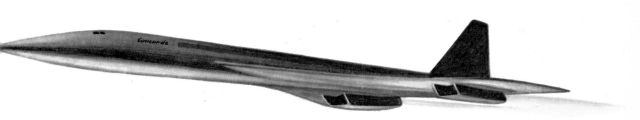

Two supersonic projects. Above: Concord, Anglo-French project; planned speed, Mach 2.2. Below: Boeing 733, United States project; planned speed, Mach 2.7.

Left: Balzac V-001, France, made its first flight in October, 1962, reaching 621 mph. Right: Experimental British hovercraft, Westland SR-N2, 1962; 3,260 horsepower; 80 mph; cruising range, 230 miles.

the experimental XP-47J version of the World War II Republic Thunderbolt fighter-bomber. The propeller itself is still in use, however. It is combined with the jet to give turbo-prop propulsion. It was really the turbo-prop (a jet that drives a propeller) that caused the piston engine to drop out of favor. The turbo-prop does not vibrate, offers more power for less weight, uses less fuel, and runs for more than 4,000 hours without overhaul. The fastest turbo-prop is the Russian Tupolev Tu-20 bomber, which has been designed to reach a speed of 590 mph at 36,000 feet. A civil version, the Tu-114 transport, has averaged 545 mph fully loaded.

Yet, following the lead of military aircraft, civil planes are turning more and more toward the pure jet engine. First there was the British Comet, the world's first commercial jetliner, then the American series of four-jet aircraft —the Boeing 707, the Douglas DC-8, the Convair, and the Coronado. Medium range aircraft have, in turn, followed the lead of their bigger counterparts. The French Sud-Aviation Caravelle, with its jets placed at the rear, has influenced designers of many other countries.

Jet aircraft have greatly reduced the time taken to cover a given distance.

In 1947, the four-engined DC-4 linked Paris with New York in 21 hours, including two stops. In 1954, the Super Constellation did it in less than 15 hours without stops, and today the Boeing 707 does the same run in seven hours. Soon, supersonic commerical aircraft will bring New York within three hours of Paris or London. Allowing for the difference of six hours in time on the two continents, the passenger leaving London at midday would arrive in New York at 9 A.M. In the other direction he would leave New York at midday and arrive in London at nine o'clock in the evening.

Quite small aircraft are now traveling faster with jet propulsion. Ten years ago, a businessman used to travel by train overnight from Boston to Washington, D.C. Now, small jet planes allow him to make a round trip and still have time for business in a day.

Amateur pilots of flying clubs are benefiting from improved engine performances, although they are using piston engines. Once restricted to a small radius around the airfield, they

United States project, Curtiss Wright X-19A, 1962; 640 mph.

can now travel much farther in light aircraft that fly as fast as a 1939 fighter.

Even gliders travel faster these days, gaining their speed from improved design and better handling techniques. Extra speed means they can stay aloft longer. By getting more quickly from one ascending zone to another, they do not lose so much height as they do in a slow crossing. Gliding records are not only those of altitude and endurance, but also of speed over a given triangular course. The record over 62 miles is 85.93 mph, set up by the German H. Linke, in a Libelle in the United States in 1967. The records over 124 and 186 miles are held by an HP-8. R. Schreder of the United States covered the 124-mile course at 67 mph in 1959, and George B. Moffat, Jr. covered the 186 miles at 74.48 mph in 1964. For 310 miles, the record is 85.25 mph, set up in 1967 by M. Jackson of South Africa in a BJ-3.

Toward Vertical Take-off

The helicopter's aerobatic ability makes it a most useful tool, but its speed is limited. If the power it used to take off vertically could be applied to forward propulsion, it could theoreti-

cally have a supersonic speed, but its shape will not allow this.

A machine that would combine the maneuverability of the helicopter and the speed of the airplane would be valuable indeed. So designers of many countries are working toward VTOL— vertical take-off and landing. Once achieved, VTOL will almost certainly result in even faster aircraft. A Mirage of 11 tons needs 6 tons of thrust to exceed Mach 2. What speed, then, can we look forward to from a plane whose total thrust will be greater than its own weight? In 1954, flights were made by the Rolls-Royce Flying Bedstead jet engine and the American Convair XFY-1 Pogo, powered by a piston engine. VTOL planes can either sit on their tails for take-off, as the Pogo does, or tilt the propellers or jets for take-off and bring them back to their normal position for forward flight.

Conventional craft are becoming more capable of STOL (short take-off and landing). The most remarkable STOL aircraft is the Breguet 941. The flow of air around the wings, caused in flight by the speed of the plane, is obtained artificially by the thrust of four propellers that take up the whole length of the wings. Flaps that point toward the ground at the same angle as the air flow give a lifting force that allows the aircraft to take off in about 600 feet. A STOL aircraft can land in places not normally accessible to airplanes, but at the same time it has a much higher speed and can carry a far greater payload than a helicopter.

Air Cushion Machines

A fascinating new family of aerial vehicles are the hovercraft, machines that ride on a cushion of air, beating all

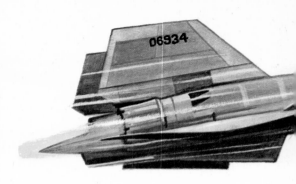

low altitude records as they do so. There are now several kinds of hover-craft, but they all work by directing a downward stream of air all around the vehicle, floating it on an air cushion and lifting it clear of the ground or water. Invented by the Englishman Christopher Cockerell in 1955, the hovercraft is equally at home traveling on land or water. The first manned craft was the SR-N1, soon followed by the SR-N2, SR-N3, and SR-N4. The SR-N1 can clear obstacles on the ground four feet high, and cross gullies four feet deep. The SR-N4 can cross a gully 20 feet deep and pass over a sheer drop of 13 feet.

Because there is no friction between the vehicle and the ground or water, speeds are much faster than any water-borne transport. The SR-N1 reached 68 knots in June, 1961. The first hover-craft in commercial use, the Vickers-Armstrong VA-3, carried its first passengers over water in July, 1962, at 60 knots. The SR-N4, the largest hover-craft, can reach 77 knots.

Hypersonic Airplanes

Supersonic flight has already been overtaken by hypersonic flight. Airline passengers are about to cross seas, oceans, and continents at Mach 2, a speed which in 1960 was reached only by experimental or secret aircraft. By 1975, thousands of passengers will have traveled at speeds once experienced only by highly trained test pilots.

The hypersonic plane will have hardly any wings at all. Should wings be needed for landing and take-off, they will be retractable. There will cer-tainly be no need for wings during flight. The wings' surface lift will have been replaced by tons of thrust, and

the faster the aircraft flies, the less carrying surface it will need. To avoid the heat barrier, the plane will have to fly at very high altitudes. As rarefied air gives less lift, the plane will have to fly at tremendous speed to compensate for this loss. The passenger of 1975 will not have the impression of flying three times as fast as the passenger of 1960, because the aircraft will be flying three or four times as high. The old aircraft bodies of duralumin will have been re-placed by ones made of stainless steel and titanium, an alloy that keeps its strength even when heated to more than 900 degrees Fahrenheit.

The French Mirage IV, the American B-58 Hustler, and the English Light-ning fly at twice the speed of sound as a matter of course. The American A-11 can fly at over 2,000 mph for two or three hours. Flights of that duration show that the speed is safe, and that designers can go to work on newer versions of the plane.

Since 1960, the American X-15 re-search aircraft has been flying at ever increasing speeds and ever higher al-titudes. Though not accepted as records because the plane is air-launched, the performances are staggering.

In June, 1962, the X-15A reached a speed of 4,104 mph (Mach 6). In Au-gust, 1963, it established an altitude record of 354,200 feet, or nearly 68 miles! The improved model, the X-15A-2 introduced in March, 1964, is

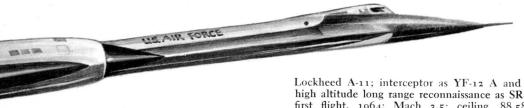

Lockheed A-11; interceptor as YF-12 A and for high altitude long range reconnaissance as SR-71; first flight, 1964; Mach 3.5; ceiling, 88,581.5 feet.

designed to fly at 5,455 mph at an altitude of 100,000 feet.

Like the A-11, the X-15 is built largely of steel and titanium. But, while the A-11 is equipped with turbo-jets, which must have air to operate and so limit the altitude at which the plane can fly, the X-15 is powered by a rocket engine, using a mixture of liquid oxygen and ammonia, which does not need atmospheric help. Ordinary rudders are useless at the great heights reached by the X-15 (there is simply no air for them to turn against) and so the craft is steered by the jet of small rockets.

The wings of the X-15 are not needed at high altitudes, but when it descends, the atmosphere starts to carry the plane again. It also starts to heat the plane up to fantastic temperatures. The nose heats to 600 degrees Fahrenheit, the windshield to 500 degrees, and the wings to 625 degrees. It is just like diving into an invisible furnace. The plane, however, is designed to withstand much higher temperatures; the wings can resist a temperature of 1,320 degrees Fahrenheit.

Rockets are the propulsion of the future, if speeds are going to be pushed even higher than those of the X-15. Ordinary jet propulsion could never reach those speeds, let alone improve on them. One possibility being investigated, which would not only give high speeds but also solve the problem of re-entry into the atmosphere, is that of the orbital glider.

This craft would be put into orbit by great rockets, which would fall away when their task was done. The remaining spaceship, shaped like a plane and not like a satellite or capsule, would re-enter the atmosphere not by falling, but by gliding; it would ricochet off the different strata of the atmosphere and lose speed with each ricochet. It would be able to choose its landing place with far greater precision than a space capsule, which is braked first by retro-rockets, then by the atmosphere itself and finally by parachute. Arriving in the atmosphere at 17,400 mph, the orbital glider would finally touch down at about 175 mph, the landing speed of a modern fighter.

North American X-15 rocket-powered research aircraft. The latest version is designated X-15A-2. In October, 1967, this model flew at 4,534 mph (Mach 6.72) to set a new unofficial speed record.

105

Speed in Space

Our century will be recorded as the one in which man escaped from the earth. In six days over Christmas, 1968, three American astronauts made a half-million-mile trip to the vicinity of the moon and back in the spaceship Apollo 8. Apollo 8 and its crew orbited the moon 10 times in 20 hours at a minimum height of 60 miles before returning to earth

At the start of the journey, after making two orbits of the earth, Apollo 8 blasted off toward the moon at a speed of 24,200 mph. On reaching the moon, its engine fired backward to reduce speed from 5,270 mph to 3,400 mph, and the craft went into moon orbit. On the return to earth, the craft accelerated from 2,395 mph to 6,000 mph to escape the moon's gravitational pull.

The re-entry into the earth's atmosphere, one of the most dangerous parts of the trip, was made at a speed of 24,630 mph. Yet by the time the craft landed in the Pacific Ocean, only 5,000 yards away from the aircraft carrier *Yorktown,* it had slowed to a mere 20 mph.

Similar speeds and slowdowns are planned for the Apollo 11 journey, except this time, the astronauts will actually land on the moon.

Astronautics: Speed v. Weight

The coming of the Space Age has meant the triumph of speed. Artificial satellites and spacecraft are already traveling at speeds almost undreamed of a few years ago. One day, perhaps, a combination of man's scientific and technical skills will allow us to travel at speeds close to the speed of light.

The terms "space" and "speed" are naturally associated in our minds. Part of the reason is that space travel, unlike travel on earth, is impossible without high speed. Although speed on earth has given us swifter and less tiring ways of communication (and hastened the advance of our civilization in the process), it has never been essential. Though it is pleasant and comfortable to travel from New York to London by Boeing, we could have got there in the end on a slow sailing ship like the *Santa Maria.*

In space flight, however, high speeds are essential if the craft is not to be pulled from its course into the gravitational field of the sun or one of the planets. The speed of a spaceship can be changed only within very narrow limits. It would be fatal, for example, to slow a spaceship down to admire the beauty of the scenery outside!

The gravity of the earth is the force that holds us down to the earth's surface. Gravity, too, gives us our weight, which is the force exerted on our body mass. One man is heavier than another simply because there is more of him for gravity to pull on. Size, or mass, determines the strength of gravitational pull. A man on the moon, for instance, would weigh one sixth of his earthly weight, even though his mass was the same, because the moon is much smaller than the earth and its gravitational pull is much weaker.

Although we do not know the nature of gravity, we do know what its effects are. Newton, and later Einstein, gave us laws of gravitational attraction. Gravity never dies away completely (the gravitational field of the earth extends throughout the whole universe), but it does get weaker with distance, until finally it can hardly be felt at all. Without this phenomenon, it would be impossible with our present rockets to send a space vehicle to the moon.

Gravitational attraction decreases in inverse ratio of the square distance. Imagine a one-pound object at sea level, that is, at the end of a radius 4,000 miles from the center of the earth. At a height of 4,000 miles *above* sea level—twice the earth's radius—the object will weigh only a quarter of its earthly weight, or four ounces. At four times the earth's radius, it will weigh a sixteenth, or one ounce, and so on. Because of this, the effort necessary to send a machine to the moon is 60 times less than if the earth's gravity remained constant through space. For all that, however, this effort is still tremendous.

Great speeds are needed to counteract the pull of the earth. In space flights, these speeds are called "velocities." Although velocity is often used in the same sense as speed, it really means speed in a given direction. It is important to grasp the difference, as it has a bearing on the space flights we shall be discussing later on. Imagine a man in a train heading north at 60 mph. Although he has a speed of 60 mph and a northward velocity of 60 mph, he has an eastward and westward velocity of 0 mph, because he is not moving in those directions. And his southward velocity is minus 60 mph. If a man stands up and walks toward the front of the train at 3 mph, he is adding his speed to that of the train, reaching a northward velocity of 63 mph and a southward velocity of minus 63 mph. If he walks at 3 mph toward the rear of the train, he then has a northward velocity of 57 mph and a southward velocity of minus 57 mph. These velocities, of course, are in relation to the ground. In relation to the train, the man walking forward would have a northward velocity of 3 mph. Walking toward the rear he would have a southward velocity of 3 mph.

Rockets that are used to put satellites into space are multistage rockets.

Incendiary rockets mounted on sticks or fired by arquebus.

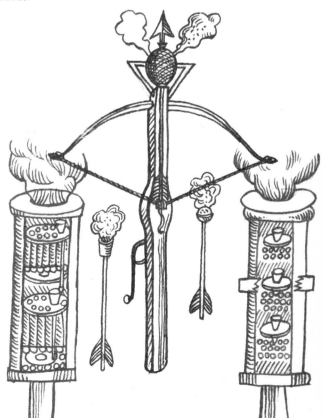

The first stage provides the gigantic thrust needed to lift the craft from the earth, straight into the air. When its fuel is spent, the first stage drops off, reducing the weight of the craft and allowing the second stage to ignite and further increase the speed.

The same thing happens with the third stage, by which time the craft is in orbit. The Saturn V, for instance, reaches a speed of 5,800 mph 2.5 minutes after lift-off, at a height of 38 miles. The second stage then takes over, and 9 minutes after lift-off it has taken the vehicle up to 110 miles at a speed of 14,200 mph. Finally, the third stage takes the vehicle up to 115 miles, gives it a speed of 17,500 mph, puts it into orbit, and shuts off 12 minutes after lift-off.

Gravity constantly pulls at the rocket, causing it to curve down toward the earth instead of shooting off into space in a straight line. A rocket with too little speed would be pulled right back to the ground. But as soon as enough speed is gained to balance the earth's pull, the rocket can circle the earth for as long as the speed is sustained. The higher the orbit, the less speed is needed to stay aloft. This is because gravity weakens in proportion to the distance from the earth. An orbit at a height of 100 miles, for instance, needs a speed of more than 17,000 mph. For an orbit at a height of 22,000 miles, a speed of 7,000 mph is enough.

The first cosmic speed is known as "orbital velocity." By increasing it, the space vehicle reaches a point where its speed causes it to shoot out of orbit away from the earth and clear of the earth's gravitational pull. The second cosmic speed is called the "escape velocity." The escape velocity of the earth is 25,000 mph, just over 7 miles a second. Once a craft is free of the gravitational pull of the earth, it goes into orbit, just as the earth does, around the sun. The earth travels around the sun with an orbital velocity of 18.5 miles per second, or 66,600 mph, and the rocket, once it is free of the earth's pull, does the same. This is because, before it left the earth, it already had the earth's orbital velocity and added its own escape velocity. This escape velocity, however, is used up in getting away from the earth, canceling it out and leaving it with only the orbital velocity around the sun it started with.

A British naval squadron bombarded Fort McHenry with rockets fired from boats in the beginning of the War of 1812.

So now the rocket is in orbit around the sun. From here the rocket can be deflected (we shall see how later) to reach other planets in the solar system. To reach the stars outside our own system, however, it would have to build up an escape velocity powerful enough to break out of the sun's gravitational pull. This third cosmic speed would mean an acceleration from earth to 14.5 miles a second, and at present there is no rocket powerful enough to do this. Another problem is that to reach a star before the astronaut was an old man, the rocket would have to travel at the speed of light. A spacecraft traveling at 25,000 mph toward the nearest star, *Alpha Centauri*, would take 115,000 years to get there!

The History of the Rocket

Because other methods of flight rely on an atmosphere for support, only the rocket is of any use in space exploration. The rocket has been with us for quite a long time—probably for more than 750 years.

The first mention of the use of rockets was in 1232, when a Chinese chronicler reported that the defenders of the town of Kai-Fung-Fu used "fire arrows" against the Mongols. Since gunpowder had been known in China since the 11th century, it is possible that rockets were used even earlier than in the siege of Kai-Fung-Fu.

Within fifty years, the rocket was in Europe, again being used in warfare. The formulas for gunpowder and plans of rockets were probably gained from the Saracens. Many of them seem to have been copied from Arab manuscripts.

Several European chronicles of the 13th and 14th centuries mention the

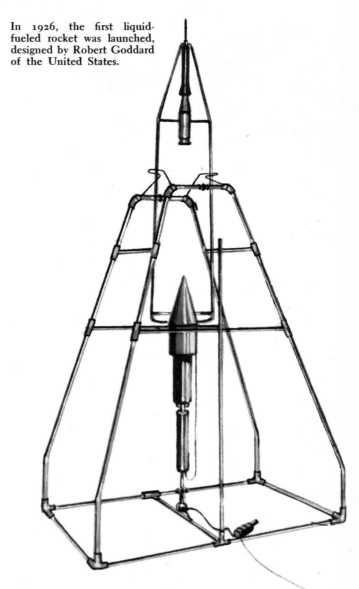

In 1926, the first liquid-fueled rocket was launched, designed by Robert Goddard of the United States.

use of war rockets. In 1379, for example, the Venetians used rockets when they fought the Genoese at the battle of the Isle of Chiozza. At the siege of Orléans in 1429, Joan of Arc had a rocket company among her troops. But toward the middle of the 16th century the progress of musketry and artillery caused the abandonment of the rocket as a weapon of war. For more than three centuries, rockets were used in Europe only for fireworks displays.

109

German V-1 of 1944. This missile, weighing 5 tons and nearly 27 feet long, could carry a warhead of 1,102 pounds at 186 mph for several hundred miles.

At the beginning of the 19th century, the rocket appeared again on the battlefields of Europe. Sir William Congreve, after the losses among British troops caused by the rockets of Tipu Sahib in India, set up a factory in London for making war rockets of his own invention. They were used by Britain with great effect during the Napoleonic Wars, and used again during the War of 1812 against the United States. Some of Congreve's rockets weighed 60 pounds and could travel 1.5 miles.

Soon other European armies began to use rockets. In Russia, especially, manufacturing methods were greatly improved. The Englishman, William Hale, made more improvements by replacing the guide stick with fins and a tail. Again, however, the gun took the lead; in 1858, the powerful and accurate rifle made the rockets of the day obsolete.

Meanwhile, inventors were looking into the possibility of a rocket-powered flying machine, but the rockets were still too primitive for any hope of success.

In 1903, a Russian schoolteacher named Konstantin Tsiolkovsky published a paper describing correctly the theory of rocket action and forecasting the use of liquid fuel. His work was not recognized until after the Revolution

of 1917, and his theories were not carried out in practice in Russia until 1933. Robert H. Goddard of the United States built and launched the first liquid-fuel rocket in 1926. In 1930, he launched a rocket that reached a speed of 500 mph and a height of 2,000 feet. As early as 1919, Goddard had forecast the landing of a rocket on the moon.

In France, work was being done by Robert Esnault-Pelterie and in Germany by Hermann Oberth. It was Germany which, during World War II, produced the most successful long-range rocket—the V-2 that was used toward the end of the war against London and Antwerp.

The rocket has had a long and violent history. Hopefully, now it will be used to allow man peacefully to explore the universe.

The Principle of the Rocket

The rocket engine is the only system of propulsion possible for space exploration. There are three main reasons for this: it can function outside the earth's atmosphere, it can reach the necessary high speeds, and the ratio between its power and its weight is the only suitable one.

The rocket engine works on the principle of reaction, defined by Newton's Third Law of Motion, which states that for every action there is an equal reaction in the opposite direction.

Every movement obeys this law. Nature gives us many examples. Animals, birds, and fish can move only by pushing against the ground, the air, or the water. The rocket, which can fly in a vacuum without apparent support from anything, would seem at first to be an exception to this law, but just the opposite is the case.

The rocket demonstrates the principle of reaction in its simplest and most direct form. Gas compressed in a closed cylinder pushes with equal force in all directions. When one end of the cylinder is opened, the gas rapidly flows out. The pressure at the closed end is now greater than the pressure at the open end, and it pushes the cylinder forward. The escaping gas is the action; the movement of the cylinder in the opposite direction is the reaction. So it is not the gas pushing against anything outside that drives the cylinder, but the gas inside pushing against the cylinder head.

The Rocket Engine

In the modern rocket, the exhaust is produced by two chemical propellants —a fuel (which burns) and an oxydizer (which allows it to burn). So it is really an internal combustion engine without any moving parts. By using its own oxidizer instead of drawing it from the air like an aircraft jet engine, the rocket is completely independent of outside atmosphere.

There are two types of propellants— liquid and solid. For centuries the makers of rockets were content to use the conventional powders, despite their limited possibilities. The coming of liquid propellants, thanks to the work of pioneers like Tsiolkovsky and Goddard, meant a real revolution. They made possible the German V-2 and then the large Russian rockets (not named by the U.S.S.R.) and American rockets, such as the American Redstone, Atlas, Thor, and Jupiter, that began the conquest of space.

Liquid propellants are dangerous to handle, often poisonous, corrosive, and above all highly explosive. Certain products must be kept at extremely low temperatures (about −297 degrees Fahrenheit for liquid oxygen). It is therefore difficult to store them, and they must be used very carefully. The rocket engine is a complicated piece of equipment. Tanks, feed pumps, tangles of piping, and a multitude of devices for regulating input and output all add to the risk of explosions caused by a failure in the mechanism.

These disadvantages of liquid propellants explain why the solids have come back into favor, now much improved over the old powders. Although less powerful than the liquids, they offer advantages such as the simplicity of the engine, reliability of performance, and the possibility of bulk storage in safety. A solid-propellant rocket can

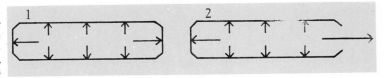

The principle of rocket propulsion: In a closed cylinder the pressure is equal all the way around (1). If an opening is made, the gas escapes, creating a thrust that puts the cylinder in motion (2).

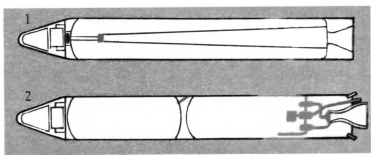

The two types of rocket engine: Solid (1) and liquid (2) propellants.

keep its charge for several months and be fired as soon as the need arises—an essential for military rockets. This is why the Minuteman and Polaris rockets use solids. In nonmilitary rockets, solid propellants are used as boosters, which assist in the launching of heavy satellites.

Thrust and Impulse

Among the measurements of performance of a rocket engine, the most important factors are thrust and specific impulse.

Thrust is the propelling force (the push of the gases) exerted on the rocket by the exhaust jet. To get off the ground, a rocket must have a thrust greater than its weight. The ratio of thrust to weight varies according to the duties of the rocket. For some military missiles it is as high as 10 to 1. On

Some early American rockets:
1. Polaris, 26 feet.
2. Jupiter and Mercury capsule, 79 feet.
3. Redstone and Mercury capsule, 83.5 feet.
4. Thor and Discoverer satellite, nearly 79 feet.
5. Atlas and Midas satellite, nearly 105 feet.
6. Saturn 1. Capable of placing up to 37,700 pounds into orbit, this large booster was used to put test versions of the Apollo spacecraft into orbit.

1   2   3   4   5   6

large satellite launching rockets, however, the ratio is about 1.25 to 1; that is, a rocket weighing 400,000 pounds fully loaded would need a thrust of 500,000 pounds. The thrust must be worked out on the total weight of the rocket before it leaves the ground. The American Saturn V, for instance, puts a payload of 260,000 pounds into earth orbit, but it needs a thrust of 7,500,000 pounds at take-off. This is because the total weight of the rocket, with its three stages and full load of fuel, is much greater than the comparatively small payload.

Specific impulse is the measure of the efficiency of the engine, and means the same in rocketry as miles per gallon does in motoring. It is the ratio of the thrust, in pounds, to the rate of fuel consumption, in pounds per second. Specific impulse is expressed in seconds and, put simply, is the length of *time* a pound of propellant would last if used at a rate that would produce a pound of thrust. Impulses of 250 seconds have been obtained with solid propellants and 300 to 350 seconds with liquid propellants.

Mass Ratio

Let us come back to the most important attribute of a rocket, its speed. The rocket accelerates all the time the engine is working. The longer the fuel lasts, therefore, the faster the rocket will travel; and the less the rocket weighs, also the faster it will travel. So rockets are designed to carry as much fuel as possible in relation to body weight. This relationship is called the mass ratio. If a rocket weighs one ton empty, and five tons fully fueled, then its mass ratio is 5 to 1. Great progress has been made on improving mass ratios. The V-2 had a mass ratio of

3 to 1. Modern space rockets have a mass ratio of as much as 10 to 1—nine tons of fuel to every ton of body weight.

The only other way of increasing a rocket's speed is to increase the speed at which the gas leaves the exhaust. But this is difficult; engineers have already got as much power from chemical propellants as it seems possible to get.

The Payload

The reason for putting a rocket into space in the first place is to take its payload up there. There would be no point at all in simply sending a lump of metal thousands of miles above the earth if it were not to be of use to us down below. The payload includes instruments, controls, radio and TV transmitters and receivers, electrical power sources, and of course the crew of a manned machine. The weight of the payload is kept down as much as possible. Today it represents only 2 to 3.5 percent of the take-off weight of a large launching rocket.

There are good reasons for this. Even under the best conditions, with an exhaust speed of 8,200 feet per second and a mass ratio of 10 to 1, no one rocket is able to exceed 12,500 mph under its own power. Why, then, are we able to put vehicles into orbit and through the space beyond, at speeds much faster than this?

The Multistage Rocket

The answer is the multistage rocket, an assembly of rockets placed one on top of the other like building blocks, which are fired in succession. As soon as one stage exhausts its fuel, it falls away from the machine (which thus gets rid of a great deal of dead weight)

and lets the next stage take over the job of propulsion. As each stage is fired, the acceleration increases, and the final stage carrying the payload has no difficulty in reaching the escape velocity of 25,000 mph.

The final speed of a multistage rocket is proportionate to the number of stages. In theory, therefore, it is possible to have unlimited speed. But engineers have come up against many delicate and complicated technical problems. So, for the time being at least, there are never more than four or five stages combined in one rocket, and even this number is only used for medium-size rockets using solid propellants.

Interplanetary Flights

We are accustomed to being earthbound. Our thinking and our habits have all been shaped by life on the surface of the globe, where the pull of gravity and friction of the atmosphere constantly impede the movement of our vehicles. Everything is reduced to a question of energy and distance. To keep up the movement of a car or an airplane, energy must be provided continuously. To cover twice the distance we must use twice the energy.

When we start our interplanetary journeys we must be prepared to change our thoughts and habits. Out in space, conditions are completely different. In terms of effort on a trip into space, only the first step really counts. The greatest effort must be provided at the start of the journey, to break the pull of gravity and the resistance of the dense atmospheric layers. In its first stage, a rocket burns up 50-65 percent of the total stock of propellant it carries.

Because the earth's gravity weakens progressively with distance, much less fuel is needed to propel the same mass once the rocket gets high above the earth. Although the mass is the same as it was on earth, the weight is much less because of the lesser gravitational pull.

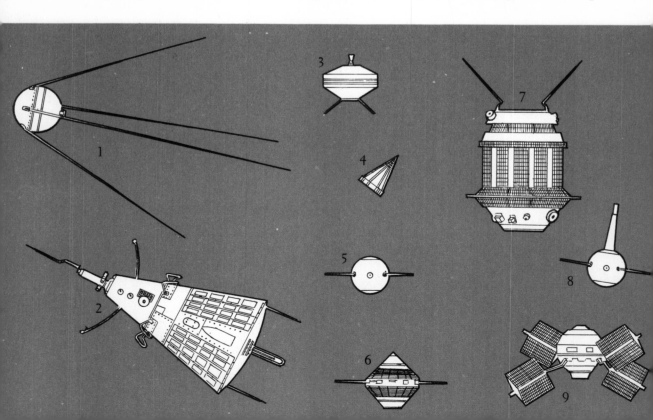

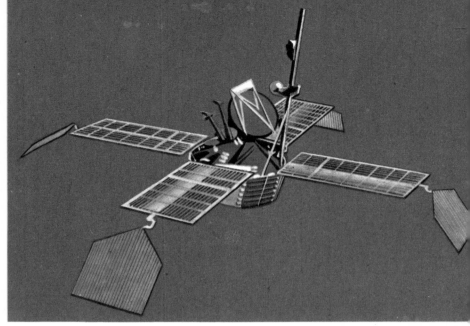

Right: Mariner 4, with solar panels and antennae ready to televise the planet Mars, July, 1965.

Below: Sixteen of more than 1,000 satellites that have been put into earth orbit or sent farther into space:
1. Sputnik 1, October, 1957.
2. Sputnik 3, May, 1958.
3. Pioneer 1, October, 1958.
4. Pioneer 3, December, 1958.
5. Vanguard 2, February, 1959.
6. Explorer 6, August, 1959.
7. Luna 2, September, 1959.
8. Vanguard 3, September, 1959.
9. Pioneer 5, March, 1960.
10. Explorer 11, April, 1961.
11. Tiros 3, July, 1961.
12. Ranger 1, August, 1961.
13. Ranger 4, April, 1962.
14. Telstar 1 (intercontinental communications satellite), July, 1962.
15. Mariner 2, August, 1962.
16. Relay 1, December, 1962.

A craft weighing four tons on earth, for example, would weigh only one ton 4,000 miles out in space.

We can say, in theory anyway, that at a certain distance from the earth, a spacecraft that has built up enough momentum will continue its flight indefinitely, obeying only inertia (the force that will keep it going unless something stops it). This theory, how-

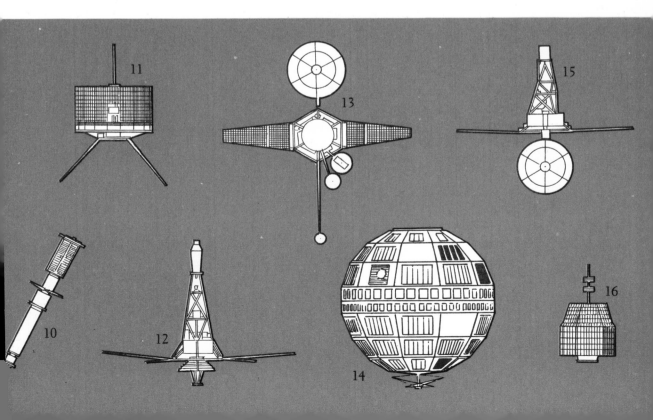

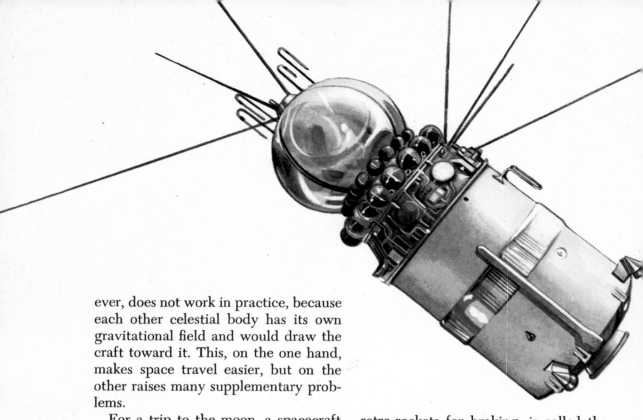

ever, does not work in practice, because each other celestial body has its own gravitational field and would draw the craft toward it. This, on the one hand, makes space travel easier, but on the other raises many supplementary problems.

For a trip to the moon, a spacecraft needs to reach the escape velocity of 25,000 mph. Although this takes it far away from the earth, it is constantly being slowed down by the earth's pull. At a distance of about 200,000 miles it has come almost to a standstill, but at this point, 20,000 miles from the moon, the pull of the moon is stronger than that of the earth. This pull gradually takes over, drawing the craft faster and faster toward the moon, either to land on its surface or to go into orbit around it. To avoid the fatal impact of landing at a speed of 1.5 miles per second, the craft would use its retro-rockets to slow down.

For the return journey, the craft will need to accelerate to a speed of only 5,400 mph (because the moon's gravity is less than the earth's) to reach the point where the earth's pull takes over again.

For a journey into space, the sum of all the velocities that have to be reached, or overcome by the use of retro-rockets for braking, is called the "characteristic velocity." This is worked out so that enough fuel can be allowed for the trip. A spacecraft coming back to earth will use the same energy in retro-rocket braking as it did to reach the escape velocity on the outward trip. The characteristic velocity would therefore be something like:

Escaping from earth:	7.0 miles per second
Landing on moon:	1.5 miles per second
Escaping from moon:	1.5 miles per second
Landing on earth:	7.0 miles per second
CHARACTERISTIC VELOCITY:	17.0 miles per second

At no time would the rocket reach this speed, but its fuel supply must be calculated as if it had to reach it, burning all its propellant in one shot. To accomplish such a feat in practice, the rocket would have to weigh on depar-

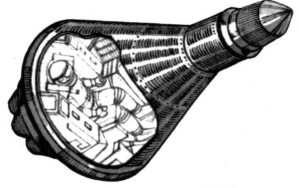

Left: Yuri Gagarin made man's first space flight in the Russian Vostok 1 on April 12th, 1961; maximum height (apogee), 198 miles; speed to reach orbit, 24,860 mph. Right: Mercury capsule Friendship VII, in which Colonel John Glenn made an orbital flight on February 20th, 1962, at a speed of 17,400 mph.

ture some 4,000 to 5,000 tons. The United States Project Apollo, which put two men on the moon on July 20, 1969, got around the technical problems involved in this by conserving fuel with a technique called "lunar-orbital rendez-vous." A three-section spacecraft arrived at the moon and went into orbit around it. Two joined sections, the command module and the service module, stayed in orbit while the lunar excursion module, the landing craft, broke away and took two of the astronauts to the moon's surface. When the astronauts were ready to return, their landing craft took them back to join up again in orbit with the other two modules. Neither their landing nor their take-off consumed as much fuel as would be necessary for the three modules together. The service module then provided the power for the return trip to earth.

Flights to the nearest planets, Mars and Venus, will be the next stages in the conquest of space. To reach Mars, the spaceship will accelerate to a speed of 7.4 miles per second (0.4 miles per second greater than the escape velocity needed) in the same direction as the earth's movement around the sun. The extra 0.4 miles per second added to the 18.5 miles per second of the earth's movement will give the craft a final speed of 18.9 miles per second around the sun. This will take it away from the earth's orbit and into the orbit of Mars.

The opposite technique will be used for a trip to Venus. The craft will be launched, again at 7.4 miles per second, but in the opposite direction to the earth's movement around the sun. The extra 0.4 miles per second is subtracted from the earth's speed, giving the spacecraft a final speed of 18.1 miles per second. The craft again moves out of the earth's orbit, being pulled nearer to the sun until it arrives in the orbit of Venus.

The maximum speed of modern rockets is about 7.5 miles per second, a

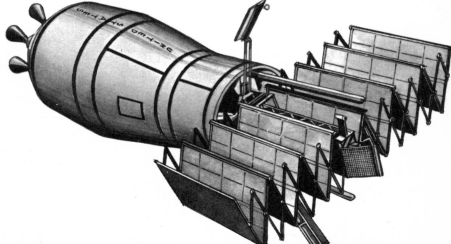

Beginning in 1965, the United States sent up a series of Pegasus satellites to gather and transmit information on meteoroids near the earth. After being placed into orbit by a Saturn I rocket, the wings open on a scissors-like system of hinged panels. The meteoroid detector panels at top and bottom are driven open by springs at the hinges.

speed nobody would have dared even to hope for ten years ago. Thanks to the techniques of adding to this speed the speed of the earth and the gravitational pull of other planets, we can already explore space dozens of millions of miles from our globe. But what does the future hold for us, and what are the limits of our ambitions?

Toward the Atomic Rocket

The chemically propelled rocket is bound to lose its monopoly as a space vehicle in the more or less near future. Its performance is limited both by the properties of its propellants and by its still-unfavorable mass ratio.

So, with bigger and bigger space projects in mind, engineers are looking into the possibilities of atomic propulsion for spacecraft. The idea can hardly fail to appeal to the designers when a pound of fissionable material contains 10,000,000 times more energy than a pound of the best chemical fuel.

The simplest solution would be to fit a space vessel with a reactor containing uranium 235. In a chemically propelled rocket, the reactor would provide only the energy, so a stock of "working fluid" or ejectable material (hydrogen,

Alexeï Leonov of the U.S.S.R., the first man to walk in space, outside Vostok II, March 19th, 1965.

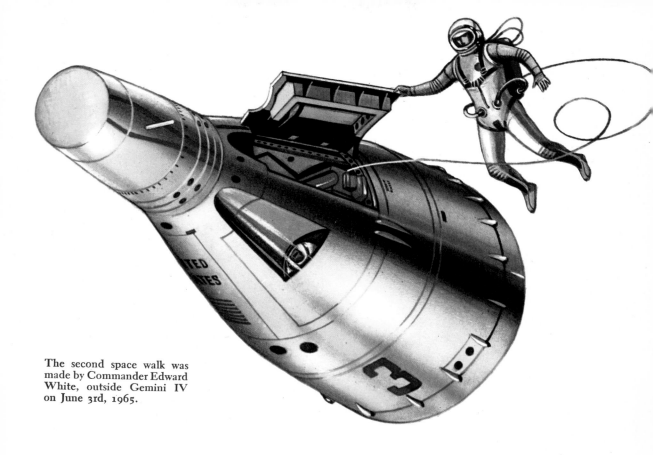

The second space walk was made by Commander Edward White, outside Gemini IV on June 3rd, 1965.

for example) would have to be carried on board. Crossing the active zone of the reactor, the working fluid would be heated to a very high temperature and then ejected by a jet pipe to create the necessary thrust. Ejection speeds would be from 5 to 7.5 miles per second, whereas with chemical propellants it is impossible at present to exceed 2.5 miles per second.

The increased ejection speed would make it possible to reduce considerably the quantity of propulsion material needed for a given mission. Because of the low density of hydrogen, however, provision would have to be made for quite large storage tanks.

Better results could be had by heating the reactor to temperatures of more than 5,400 degrees Fahrenheit, but the difficulty here would be in finding a material capable of withstanding such fierce heat. One answer lies in the gas reactor. A mixture of uranium and hydrogen would be injected into the combustion chamber, so that the fluid would be heated directly by the fission fragments. This method, however, would be very expensive because the uranium, which is rare and costly, would be ejected with the hydrogen. Scientists are now working on ways of separating the two, so that when the hydrogen is ejected, the uranium stays behind.

These are just a few of the problems facing the designers working on atomic propulsion, but they serve to show the difficulties involved. In the United States, research and ground trials have been going on for several years, but the first nuclear propelled rocket (RIFT) will not be launched for several years to come.

The Apollo 8 flight, the first manned journey to the moon, was accomplished in December, 1968.

1. Apollo 8 lifts off from Cape Kennedy and at 115 miles altitude enters earth orbit.
2. After two revolutions, the third stage is fired. The capsule leaves earth orbit at a speed of 24,640 mph.
3. The capsule separates from the third stage.
4. The third stage starts toward the sun, where it will go into orbit.
5. At 29,790 miles from the moon, the capsule enters the moon's gravitational field.
6. The capsule's rocket is fired, and it goes into orbit around the moon at 3,611 mph.
7. It makes two high lunar orbits and, after firing one of its rockets, 8 circular orbits 69.4 miles from the moon's surface.
8. Return trip: Rockets fired at 6,014 mph carry the capsule out of the moon's gravity.
9. Capsule enters earth's gravitational field and reaches 24,552 mph.
10. The capsule re-enters the earth's atmosphere.
11. Slowed by parachutes, it splashes down in the Pacific Ocean.

Two other problems are weight and contamination of the atmosphere. The instruments and crew will have to be protected from radiation by thick armor-plating. RIFT also could be used only at high altitudes; atomic waste sprayed into our atmosphere would be highly dangerous to humanity. RIFT would therefore be sent up as the third stage of the launch vehicle.

One day, when man becomes able to push on to the stars, even the nuclear rocket will probably become obsolete. We have seen already how long it would take a present-day spacecraft to reach the nearest star, *Alpha Centauri*. Even light, traveling at 186,000 miles a

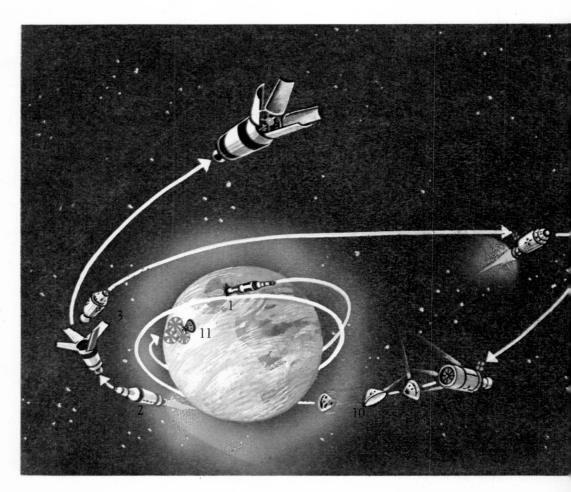

second, takes four years to get from *Alpha Centauri* to earth. The answer to journeys across such distances seems to be to build a machine that would travel at the speed of light.

In theory, this is possible with a photon rocket. A photon is a unit of electromagnetic radiation produced by collisions between atomic nuclei or electrons. If this reaction were to be achieved in the combustion chamber of a missile, the photons could be reflected by a large mirror and ejected to create the thrust. Although the mass of a photon is incredibly small, its speed is prodigious.

So much for the theory. The difficulty in practice would be that the photon rockets would take three or four years to accelerate to the speed of light, and as long again to slow down. The rocket would have to do this, anyway, for the sake of the crew. The human body can bear accelerations of more than 10 or 15g only for very short periods. (g is the force of gravity at the earth's surface, equal to an acceleration of 32 feet per second. A rocket accelerating at 10g would be increasing its speed by 320 feet every second.) This is not really an insuperable problem, providing that astronauts of the future are willing to spend ten or twenty years on a journey.

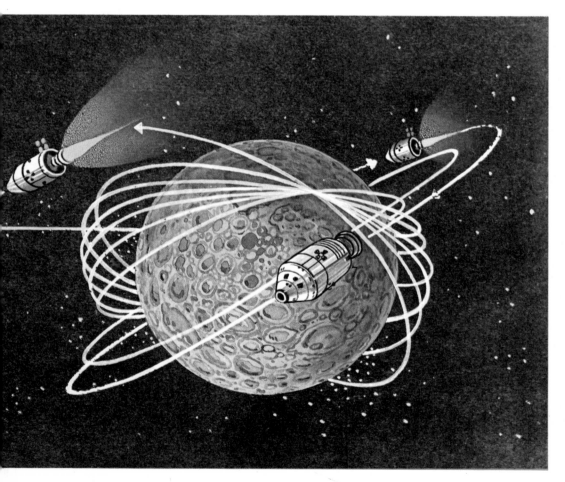

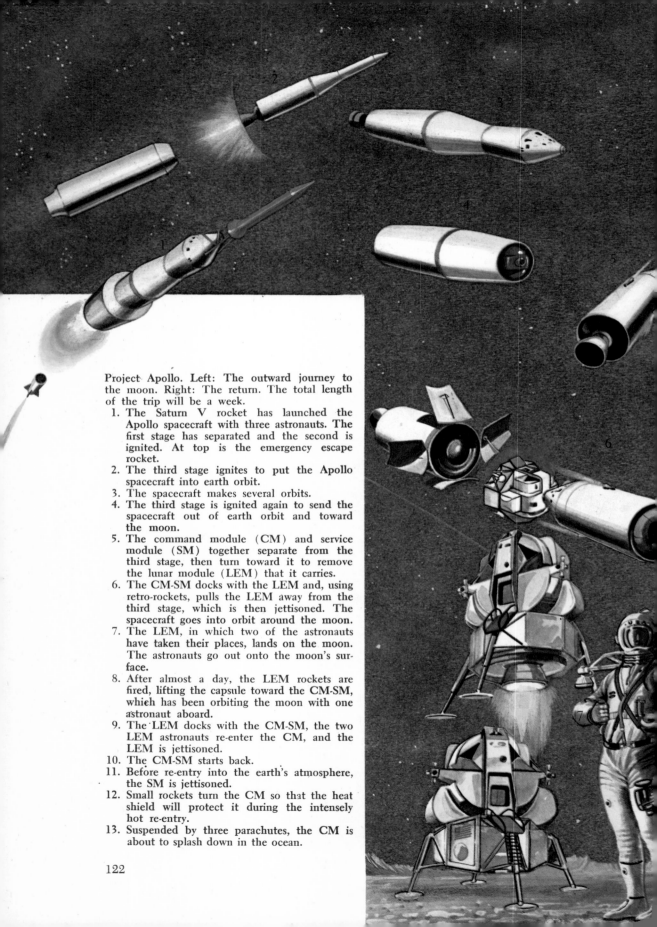

Project Apollo. Left: The outward journey to the moon. Right: The return. The total length of the trip will be a week.

1. The Saturn V rocket has launched the Apollo spacecraft with three astronauts. The first stage has separated and the second is ignited. At top is the emergency escape rocket.
2. The third stage ignites to put the Apollo spacecraft into earth orbit.
3. The spacecraft makes several orbits.
4. The third stage is ignited again to send the spacecraft out of earth orbit and toward the moon.
5. The command module (CM) and service module (SM) together separate from the third stage, then turn toward it to remove the lunar module (LEM) that it carries.
6. The CM-SM docks with the LEM and, using retro-rockets, pulls the LEM away from the third stage, which is then jettisoned. The spacecraft goes into orbit around the moon.
7. The LEM, in which two of the astronauts have taken their places, lands on the moon. The astronauts go out onto the moon's surface.
8. After almost a day, the LEM rockets are fired, lifting the capsule toward the CM-SM, which has been orbiting the moon with one astronaut aboard.
9. The LEM docks with the CM-SM, the two LEM astronauts re-enter the CM, and the LEM is jettisoned.
10. The CM-SM starts back.
11. Before re-entry into the earth's atmosphere, the SM is jettisoned.
12. Small rockets turn the CM so that the heat shield will protect it during the intensely hot re-entry.
13. Suspended by three parachutes, the CM is about to splash down in the ocean.

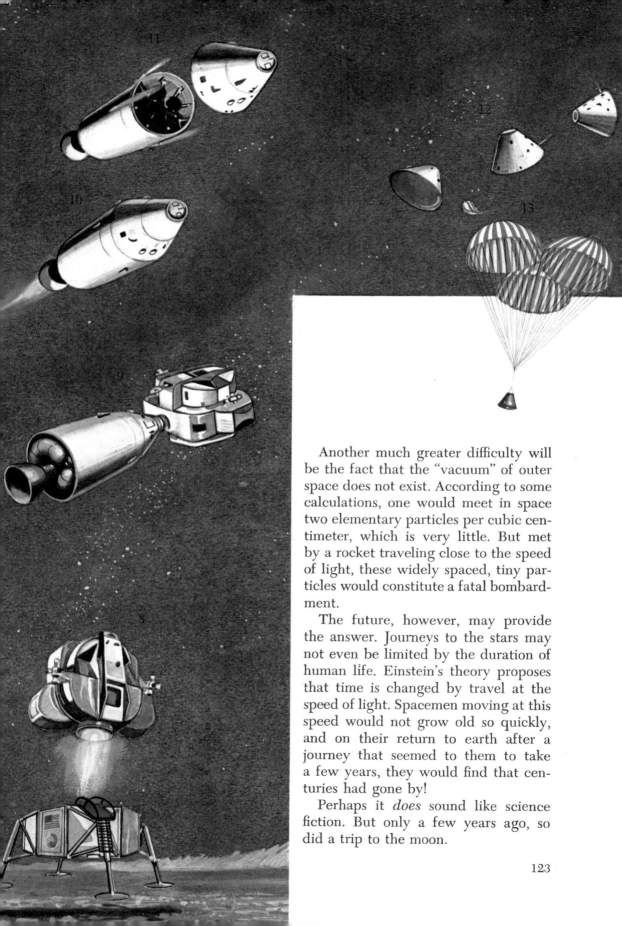

Another much greater difficulty will be the fact that the "vacuum" of outer space does not exist. According to some calculations, one would meet in space two elementary particles per cubic centimeter, which is very little. But met by a rocket traveling close to the speed of light, these widely spaced, tiny particles would constitute a fatal bombardment.

The future, however, may provide the answer. Journeys to the stars may not even be limited by the duration of human life. Einstein's theory proposes that time is changed by travel at the speed of light. Spacemen moving at this speed would not grow old so quickly, and on their return to earth after a journey that seemed to them to take a few years, they would find that centuries had gone by!

Perhaps it *does* sound like science fiction. But only a few years ago, so did a trip to the moon.

123

Index

126